Published in the United States of America
By Family Solutions Publishing, LLC

All scripture references are
King James Version unless
Otherwise indicated

Book Design by: FSI Publishing, Inc.

Printed in the United States of America by
Family Solutions Publishing, LLC
1716 West State Highway 152
Mustang, Oklahoma 73064
success@familysolutions.info

Publisher's Cataloging in Publication

Tate, Ryan and Christy

To Tie the Knot or Not / Ryan and Christy Tate

Originally published: Oklahoma City: Family Solutions Publishing:2003

Includes Bibliographical references

1.Spiritual life– protestant 2. Marriage 3. Family

ISBN 0-9740939-0-4 $14.95

First Printing: March 2003

By

http://www.familysolutions.info

To Tie The Knot Or Not?

Principles You Must Master Before You Marry

By

Ryan and Christy Tate

FOREWORD

We have all referred to marriage at one time or another as, ***"tying the knot."*** Not until we started writing this book about the principles that guided us when we were dating and engaged did we actually ask ourselves about its meaning. The title we chose for this book, ***"To Tie The Knot Or Not,"*** originated from questions so many young people at our seminars have asked us about relationships with their boyfriends or girlfriends. They ask, "Ryan and Christy, I am so confused about what I should do about getting married, I'm not sure this person is the one - should I *tie the knot, or not?*" The next eleven chapters you are about to read are for every person on the planet who has ever asked that question.

The phrase, ***"to tie the knot,"*** had its origin in Ireland, Scotland, and England in the 15th Century. A ceremony called, "hand fasting," would take place between couples that wished to be married. They would call together their family, friends, and clergyman. The clergyman would have the couple cross hands and would place an untied rope across their wrists as he made several challenges to them about the seriousness of their consideration. He and the assembled audience would then declare for that year and one day the couple would be committed to working toward the potential of a life-long relationship.

After the year and a day had passed, the group would again assemble. If the couple announced their decision *not* to marry, the cleric would ceremonially remove the untied rope from their wrists and declare that they would go their own way with ***"no strings attached"*** (another common phrase we derived from this custom). However, if they announced their desire to wed, he would take the rope, wrap it several times around their wrists, and formalize the marriage by tying a knot in the rope after the couple had completed a series of eighteen vows. During the celebration that followed, they would remain tied to one another as a symbolic gesture of their decision. They had ***"tied the knot."***

As you make"*your* decision regarding a potential life partner, think carefully about every step. It may take you a year and a day or ten years and a day, but *whatever* your time frame, make sure you have thought it through clearly before you stand before the minister and ask him to ***"tie the knot!"*** Our prayer is that this book about *our* journey to that decision will help you with yours.

Ryan and Christy Tate

Oklahoma City, Oklahoma 2003

DEDICATION

To Trinity, my (Ryan's) sister for whom I pray each day that God will bring into your life a man who deserves you, loves you, and respects you as much as I do.

To my (Christy's) brothers Joe and Tim, may the principles in this book guide you to the rich blessings of Godly wives who will fill your lives with joy and success. We love you all and dedicate this book to each of you.

-Ryan and Christy

CONTENTS

Tightening the Rope

Tying the Knot

INTRODUCTION

An ounce of prevention is worth a pound of cure.

-Benjamin Franklin

In November of last year (2002) Christy and I were speaking in Tulsa, Oklahoma to a group of about 1,500 students at a local college. At the completion of the seminar a young lady came up to us and asked if she could speak with us for a moment. We stepped away from the rest of the crowd in order to hear clearly what she had to say.

The young lady had just turned sixteen years old and began to tell us about how she was pregnant and living with her aunt and uncle. Then she asked a question that motivated us further to write this book. This sixteen year old asked us if we thought it would be good for her to move in with her eighteen year old boyfriend and live with him until they could afford to get married. I can still remember the look on Christy's face, and I could read her thoughts. The young pregnant girl was nowhere near capable of caring for herself, let alone providing for a child. She was a child herself!

Christy and I were able to truly minister and witness to this young lady and direct her in the path that God has chosen for her life. I thank God and know that if for no other reason he brought us there for her.

It was this experience and others like it that caused Christy and me to realize our society must begin to view marriage as a sacred union once again; the perfect image of Christ and the church. Marriage is a gift from God, a lifelong commitment to another person, not a quick fix to your current situation. All across our nation divorce rates are climbing to heights we have never seen before. Why? It is simple; there is a lack of preparation and knowledge when it comes to marriage. Later on we will discuss more about marriage preparation and principles to live by when thinking about marriage. Benjamin Franklin once said, " An ounce of prevention is worth a pound of cure!" If we want to see divorce rates change, then society must embrace seriously once again the marriage vow "till death do us part." Young adults, teenagers, and unmarried persons must not rush the second most important decision they will make in their life after salvation.

The fact that you have picked up this book and begun to read is clear indication that you are thinking about this decision. *Should I get married? Maybe the single life is best for me?* Maybe you have never been married and are still optimistic you might find "Mr. or Mrs. Right." Possibly you have been married once, or twice - and are thinking about taking that step again. We would like to encourage you to allow God to be part of your decision. Seek out the true desires of your heart and take a look at who you are and the principles in this book before rushing into anything.

We are constantly amazed at how many young people and couples wanting to get married overlook all the problems they have and tell us that they are in love and that will get them by. Love is not enough! Commitment, along with planning and preparation is what will make a marriage succeed. Newsflash! Marriage is work – and much harder than anyone thinks.

Many couples think that once they get married all of their problems will just go away and they will live in complete happiness with a beautiful house surrounded by a white picket fence and a romantic fire always burning in the fireplace. This is an unrealistic expectation.

In high school I (Ryan) played just about every sport possible, but one of my favorites was football. I was a strong safety and because of that position I was to stop the run first, and cover the pass second. I loved to come up and smack any ball carrier at the line of scrimmage. It brought me a lot of personal enjoyment and pleasure. The only problem was that I would get in such a habit of running toward the line to make the tackle that all the opposing quarterback had to do was drop a short pass over the line where I was *supposed* to be and *viola*, the opposing team would get first down after first down if not more. I'll never forget as one of my coaches sat me down and said, "Ryan, I know you love to make big hits, but you're killing us by not stopping the pass. I need you to start sacrificing temporary pleasure for long term happiness." I never thought of it that way before. Instead of being selfish and always trying to make the big play I needed to do what was right. Doing this would benefit my entire team and I personally could experience even more success.

When it comes to marriage, pre-marital sex, and living together before marriage one simple rule can make the outcome more positive for everyone; sacrifice temporary pleasure for long term happiness. If men and women would begin to make this decision, the divorce rate would drop, statistics for teenage pregnancies would be lowered, underage drinking and drug abuse numbers would fall, and many other negatives that affect our society would change dramatically. Remember, marriage doesn't fix anything, while it is an amazing blessing from God; marriage is a whole new batch of problems and questions. We must have a complete understanding of God's desire for us and his Word before marriage. If you try to achieve your goals without a complete understanding of God's word and His plan for marriage you are doomed to failure. God's Word is now and always the only true standard for success. Proverbs 24:3 affirms God's desire for starting a home, *"Through wisdom is an house built; and by understanding it is established."*

People respond to information in different ways, however basic information needs to be examined. We must know what God says, obey Him and trust His Word as we apply each principle to our own personal circumstances. It will produce His intended results. Faithful trust is the key!

You may be wanting more meaningful dating relationships. You could be thinking about "tying the knot" for the first time, or you are considering repeating that decision again. Whatever your circumstance, consider the principles we have outlined in this book as critical to your success and remember - God has *called* you to succeed!

CHAPTER ONE

All By Myself...

Be Content With Yourself

All By Myself...

Be Content With Yourself

"Now Godliness with contentment is great gain."
-I Timothy 6:6 NKJ

But no man, woman, or child can appease this longing; it can only be satisfied by the ultimate Bridegroom, Christ Jesus.
-Jones and Kendall, Lady In Waiting

For a dating and relationship book it might come as a surprise to you that Christy and I (Ryan) would begin by discussing the importance of knowing who you are individually, regardless of anyone else in your life. Current society and media trends place huge emphasis on the importance of having someone in your life. The theme that "you're nobody" unless you have "somebody" is a common selling point for advertisers everywhere. Nearly all the new reality television shows place this same emphasis as the core of their plot. Recently, Christy and I saw the television commercial for a new show where America chooses a guy and a girl by telephone vote to marry. The couple will not meet until the day of their wedding! We can only imagine where that marriage is headed.

It is imperative, before another person shares your life, that you are content with who *you* are. Are you emotionally healthy and whole? Are you satisfied with where you are spiritually? When Christ commanded us to *"love our neighbors as ourselves"* (Matthew 19:19), He was basically giving us permission to love ourselves – not in a proud or boastful way, but to have a deep inner peace that we are special to God. Your first priority is to be the man or woman who pleases God.

It is extremely important to remember that it is *good* to desire that special someone in your life. This is a natural and appropriate desire. Genesis 2:18 says, *"And the Lord God said, 'It is not good that a man should be alone; I will make him a helper comparable to him.."* At creation God could have simply created man, but He didn't. He chose to make a woman for the man. God could have made woman from the dirt or any other element of his choosing, but He chose to create the woman from man's flesh and bone, demonstrating how man and woman become one flesh in marriage. *"Therefore a man shall leave his father and mother and be joined to his wife, and they shall become one flesh,"* (Genesis 2:24). God *intended* for us to marry and share our lives with someone. It is good to desire someone of the opposite sex, with whom you may share your life.

Marriage is an amazing blessing when done correctly, and the right way is God's way. Marriage can also be a curse and one of the most difficult and troublesome experiences of your life when done the wrong way, not God's way!

You see, God wants an intimate relationship with YOU. Our concern doesn't need to be where to find someone to marry; we need to concern ourselves with our relationship with Jesus. Don't ever underestimate the power of prayer when it comes from the heart. If it is a husband or wife you desire then remain close to God and pray that whomever He chooses for you will come into your life. Philippians 4:6 says, *"Be anxious for nothing, but in everything by prayer and supplication, with thanksgiving, let your request be made known to God."* God cares about what we want and has someone perfect for you. Submit your request to Him and begin to praise Him for the answer.

When I (Ryan) was thirteen years old I began to pray for my future wife. Every night before I went to sleep I would simply pray that God would protect and bless her. I had no name to use so it was a very general prayer. As I grew older I began praying for the same protection, but that God would bring her into my life. My parents joke that while I was busy praying my future wife *into* my life they were praying a couple of girlfriends *out* of my life. I thank God for their prayers and concerns, and today I have the perfect wife for me!

I can still remember the day that I knew I wanted to marry Christy. It was the most wonderful, amazing feeling I had ever known. Not the butterflies getting ready to jump out of my stomach, but a peace that made my choice clear. From that point on I was able to pray for Christy by name. However, this experience I had and the amazing wife that God had chosen for me did not come without sacrifice. Had I been preoccupied or desperate just to have someone, anyone, I doubt that God's true intension for a wife would have come to me.

As we live our lives and become anxious to meet that special someone, we tend to take things into our own hands and try to create what we think is right for us. We try to "make" the person the right one, whether they are or not. This often ends in disappointment and heartache. We can't do better than God, but He can't work in our lives and bless us if we keep getting in the way. By reading this book you are asking, "What is the best way to find Mr. or Mrs. Right?" The answer is simple! Follow Jesus Christ with your life and live for Him. Concern yourself with being in the Word and prayerfully trust God to direct you to the one He is preparing for you. Let Him do the rest. We speak from experience when we say that it will happen when you least expect it.

During my first semester of college I (Christy) was sitting in my dorm room reading and praying when I felt God speaking to my heart. It was August 13, 1997 and He was telling me not to enter a dating relationship for a year. Up to this point I was the type of person who always had to have someone. I felt affirmed, more desirable when someone wanted me. It made me feel better about myself to simply have someone. The problem was that I could never find what I wanted so I was constantly trying to fix people - make them go to church, read the Bible and so on. So when the Holy Spirit was telling me to refrain from dating for an entire year, my first thought was, "Yeah right."

Through prayer and faithfulness I set out to follow God's desire. I can still remember thinking to myself that there was no way I could do it, especially for an entire year. As time passed, the days turned to weeks, weeks turned to months, then suddenly, I realized a year had passed. It was amazing! Instead of going out on a Friday night, I had a date with God. That was my answer when friends asked what I was doing over the weekend. Over the course of that year I grew closer to God than I had ever been. I found myself not needing relationships and actually not even desiring to be in one. You see I had Jesus and He was all that I desired.

After that year passed I believed that God was happy with me and on August 13, 1998 I got on my knees to pray when the Holy Spirit spoke to my heart again. You guessed it, God was asking for another year. This time I was less reluctant to turn myself over to Him because of the growth I had experienced over the last year. I dedicated myself to serving Him and only dating Him for another year. This too was one of the best years of my life. My relationship, trust, and faith in God as well as my knowledge of the Word grew immensely. I had completely turned myself over to Him.

Before I knew it another year had passed. Two years without being in a relationship, I couldn't believe I had made it.

On August 13, 1999 I knelt to pray and the Holy Spirit spoke to me again, only this time I felt a release. I had the clear indication that it was okay for me to date. My first reaction was "NO!" This decision had become a lifestyle for me. "I only want you Lord!" Looking back I know that God knew He had me forever. It had been a test of faithfulness. During those two years of *dating God* I had raised my standard! Any man would have to pass through God to get to my heart. I was completely confident because I knew who I was in Christ and I knew that He loved me more than anyone on earth could *ever* love me.

During that time, God changed the desires of my heart to match His. If you spend enough time with Him, He will do just that. It wasn't long until God blessed me with one of the most amazing miracles of my life. He brought my husband, Ryan Tate, into my life. Ryan was everything that I had ever desired in a husband and more. Each day, now in our married life, God reveals to me another reason why *He* chose Ryan. However, it took my willingness to choose God first, before He brought Ryan into my life. God didn't simply want me to prove myself to Him, although He is blessed by our willingness to spend time with Him. He also wanted to work on my life. If I had met Ryan and married him without spending the time God had asked me to spend with Him, I *know* I would not be the type of partner or wife that I am today.

God not only used those two years to help me grow closer to Him, but he also used those years to make me a better person. I'm not saying that everyone has to do what God asked of me. I don't know how God will lead you. For me it was two years, for you it might be two weeks, for the Israelites in the Old Testament it was 40 years of wandering in the desert. I *do* know God wants to be involved in this part of your life, and the only way to experience true happiness in relationships and marriage is to follow Christ and let Him have all of you.

CHAPTER TWO

Hooked on a Feeling...

Love vs. Infatuation

Hooked on a Feeling...

Love vs. Infatuation

"The heart is deceitful above all things."

- Jeremiah 17:9 NKJ

Many relationships spring from just loving the *idea* of being in love when it isn't real love at all.
–Richard and Rita Tate

LOVE

How do I love thee? Let me count the ways. I love thee to the depth and breadth and height my soul can reach…

-Elizabeth Browning

There are different kinds of love – there's love for parents and family, love for close friends, love for sports, pets, and romantic love. The word "love" in the English language has several variations in the original Greek. We want to discuss three with you.

The first word for love in the Greek is *agape*. Agape love is the love God has for us. It is spiritual and supernatural. The second word for love is *philos*. This may sound a bit familiar, considering the city of Philadelphia is the city of "brotherly love." This type of love is the kind of love you have for a friend, brother, or sister. The last word for love is *eros*. Eros is the type of love we will be discussing mostly throughout this chapter. Eros is romantic love and is the love that a husband and wife share in marriage (this is where the word, erotic originated). Eros is the type of love designed for one person, your future husband/wife.

As you try to separate love and infatuation you will find some important truths will emerge. You don't have to be "in love" in order to be in a fruitful relationship. Love isn't something that happens right away. It takes time – it grows and builds over time. You may start out caring about someone and then have those feelings develop into love, or the opposite, feelings will disappear. You may realize that your relationship with that person may have great benefit but will never become a life-long commitment.

Love is not just sexual desire. Our culture has taught us that sex and love are one and the same. Television, movies, and magazines continuously promote this lie. Sex is a beautiful God-given activity that is wonderful when practiced within the boundaries of a Biblical marriage. Sex is the completion of the binding of two people within Biblical marriage; it is a God given gift. But there is much more to love than sexual attraction alone.

CHARACTERISTICS OF TRUE LOVE

- There is no jealousy in the relationship
- There is no alcohol and substance abuse
- You are never asked to compromise your moral values
- You are truthful and open with one another
- You keep your promises and commitments
- You practice the same faith
- You both agree that marriage is a covenant which is designed to last forever
- Your family and friends approve of your relationship
- You refrain from using manipulation
- You are willing to give up and share power in decision making

- You don't allow sex to be the bond of your relationship
- You respect the person

True love is not about power, obsession or dependence. People who truly love each other do not try to control each other and they do not try to change each other. Real love is best seen as devotion and action, not as emotion. Love is not exclusively based on how we feel. Certainly our emotions are involved, but they cannot be our only criteria for love. True devotion will always be the natural result of true love.

INFATUATION

Infatuation is fleeting desire – it is one set of glands calling to another.

-Ann Landers

It is easy to confuse love with other feelings, sometimes referred to as a crush or infatuation. Feelings that accompany infatuation can often be very powerful, and there is nothing innately wrong with them. They are normal and you will likely experience them many times in life, but look closely at the differences between love and infatuation.

HOW CAN YOU TELL THE DIFFERENCE BETWEEN LOVE AND INFATUATION? [1]

1. Do you have a lot of fear of losing each other?
2. When you think of the other person is your first thought a physical attraction?
3. Do you get lonely and depressed when they are not around, even for short periods of time?
4. Do you get weak in the knees and butterflies in the stomach when you are with them?
5. Is it hard to be happy when they are not around?

If you answered, "yes" to three or more of the previous five questions then be careful. You are probably working on infatuation instead of the real thing. Satan loves to disguise real love with infatuation, which is a close but cheap counterfeit. Infatuation usually is a result of one's own insecurity and need for affirmation. Satan knows this and will try to confuse you by making you think it's love when actually you're only attracted physically or emotionally to the person. Make sure your relationship is secured in God's love before you make any commitment.

ASK YOURSELF AN IMPORTANT QUESTION. AM I IN LOVE OR IN LUST?

Remember, infatuation is a feeling and real love requires a commitment. Infatuation is just a love of *emotion.* Real love, though, is love of *devotion.* Only the emotions are affected in infatuation, but in real love both the emotions and the will are involved. A person "falls into" infatuation but "grows into" love.

Real love is primarily interested in the other person. It seeks to give instead of get. Love seeks the good of the other person. The best example of love is in the person of Jesus Christ. If *"Jesus is...the truth"* (John 14:6) and *"God is love"* (I John 4:16), then true love can only be seen in being like Him.

Infatuation has no lasting qualities that real love possesses. It is weakened by time and separation where real love is strengthened by time and separation. This does not mean that there will be no pain in separation. To the contrary, there is great pain in separation if you are truly in love.

Feelings of insecurity are revealed in infatuation-based relationships. You are excited and eager but not genuinely happy. There are nagging doubts, unanswered questions, little bits and pieces about the relationship you would just as soon not examine too closely. It might spoil the dream. Love, however is friendship that has caught fire. It takes root and grows one day at a time. It gives you strength and grows beyond you to bolster the one you love. You are warmed by their presence, even when they are not with you. Infatuation says you must get married right away or you might lose them! Love says be patient and don't panic. Love plans the future with confidence. Infatuation focuses on sexual excitement, and when you are together you hope it will end in sexual intimacy. Love says you must be friends before you will ever be lovers. Love waits for sexual intimacy in marriage. Infatuation lacks confidence and trust, and love MEANS trust. Do not use the word love until you know it is the real thing and it is God's time to reveal it. In fact…

NEVER TELL A PERSON YOU LOVE THEM UNLESS YOU ARE WILLING TO MARRY THEM.

"Father God,

...Ryan has shown me a picture of You that I've never seen. You are so beautiful in him. You have blessed me through him with the rarest blessing of all – true love, that's Your kind of love because You are True and You are Love – so True Love is God and Jesus... and that is what Ryan gives me. Let me never give him anything less. Be the Standard of my love for him. I do love him Lord – You did perfect (of course). He is so much like You. He's so much like his Father (You). Let me never let Ryan be anything less. I love him; always be with us... "

-An excerpt from Christy's prayer book shortly after engagement

CHAPTER THREE

Who Wrote The Book Of Love...

God's Blueprint for Dating

Who Wrote The Book Of Love...

God's Blueprint For Dating

"A man's heart devises his way: but the Lord directs his steps."

– Proverbs 16:9 NKJ

You take the tone of, and become like, the company you are in.
- The Earl of Chesterfield, 1742

Throughout my (Christy's) high school and college years I worked as a waitress at Metro Diner, a 50's restaurant in Tulsa, OK. Great tortilla soup! I absolutely loved the people, the music, and the work. Consequently, there were some bad days as well. Usually resulting from dropped food or wrong orders (of course it was never my fault). Here's how it was supposed to work. I would take the person's order, then relay the information to the cook. This is where most problems occurred. The order would either be misplaced, misunderstood, even dropped on the floor, or the cook just simply failed to read it. However it happened, sometimes the customer would get the wrong food, or it would be late. Sorry!

In Psalm 37:23, God says that He has ordered the steps of a good man. Picture God placing an order on your life. My order might have read, "I would like her be born to Richard and Julie Kelley and come to know me at an early age. Then have her marry Ryan Tate, have children…" and so forth.

Throughout our lives it is up to us to get the order right. I Corinthians 2:9-10 says that, *"Eye has not seen, nor ear heard, nor have entered into the heart of man the things which God has prepared for those who love Him. But He has revealed them to us through His Spirit."* We must listen to His Spirit, just as the cooks at Metro had to listen to the order. Give your best effort to prepare the order He reveals to you through His Holy Spirit. Think of how enjoyable it will be at the feast He has prepared for you. Then listen carefully for the instructions on preparing the dish He desires from you.

A lot of people keep their problems and get rid of their partner and only end up having the same issues with the next person.

–Diane Plumberg

10 GUIDELINES FOR SUCCESSFUL DATING

1.Don't look for a date

"But seek first the Kingdom of God and His righteousness, and all these things shall be added unto you."

– Matthew 6:33 NKJ

Ever try to make a parakeet sit on your finger by poking at the bird or trying to catch him in your hand first? – total havoc in the bird cage. How different it–was when you simply held your finger still and let the parakeet come to you. Moral —*don't get desperate.* Trust God and you will be in the right place at the right time. Let God bring the dating relationship to you.

In the Old Testament of the Bible men and women left it up to their fathers to find their mate – want to try that today? Times and cultures have changed but what a perfect picture of trusting a father.

We should have no less trust in our–*heavenly* Father than people in the Old Testament had in their *earthly* fathers. Give God your heart, seek Him first, and make your requests known to Him. Then, simply rest in the fact that He has "ordered your steps."

2. Define your reasons for dating

Insanity is doing the same thing over and over again but expecting different results.

– John Baker, Celebrate Recovery

You probably observe some of your friends dating the wrong kind of person again and again. Why are they opening themselves up for pain and disappointment over and over? Perhaps they have never determined why or exactly who they *should* date.

Defining your reasons for dating is probably one of the easiest principles to master. It's easy because *you* make all the rules. Ryan always says to simply grab a sheet of paper and draw a line down the center. Write what you want in a mate on one side, and on the other side write what you don't want in someone. The key is sticking to your list.

Many times we enter a relationship, not liking the person, but the potential the person has. For example, if you want to marry an astronaut, date only astronauts. What we tend to do is date the first person who comes along and try to fit them in a space suit. You may squeeze them in, but it will be a painful and miserable process. God says He will give you the desires of your heart, but He can only do that if you define them and *stick* to them.

The reason we put ourselves in the same relationship over and over again is because nothing is changing. If nothing changes, you will continue to get the same results. Decide what you want and change whatever needs to be changed in order to meet that type of person.

One area to check yourself in is *where* you are meeting people. Place is everything. This is because places have reputations. You're clothing changes, your body language changes, and sometimes your attitude changes too. Two people meeting at a club on a Saturday night will more than likely start their conversation off differently than if they met the next morning at church. Where you meet is almost as important as whom you meet, because it can define the relationship. Start your relationships in a place where you can be proud.

3. Work on being a good *friend*, not a good boyfriend or girlfriend.

"A friend loves at all times"

– Proverbs 17:17 NKJ

Obviously from the physical anatomy given at only a few weeks after conception, I (Ryan) do not have to work at being a male. With Christy it is the same. She does not have to work at being a female. She just is. We do say that relationships are not always easy, but we think everyone pretty much has this part covered. Whether male or female, the basics of good friendships remain the same. Words like honest, loyal, sensitive, and respectful come to mind when describing good friends. How does this apply to dating?

Eliminating the first half of the words boyfriend and girlfriend takes a lot of pressure off of the already difficult task and it is much easier to just be you. The lasting relationships are the ones based on friendship, not on sexuality. So it only makes since to focus and strive for excellence in this area.

You must keep in mind too a particular verse. Proverbs 27:6 says, *"Faithful are the wounds of a friend, but the kisses of an enemy are deceitful."* Friendship is not mere flattery and fun times. Friendship is a constant act of love (see chapter two, love or infatuation). Good friends rebuke in love and look out for God's best for you. Strive to be this kind of friend, especially in dating relationships.

4. Commit to treating your date how you want other people to treat your future husband or wife

Do unto others, as you would have others do unto you.

– Golden Rule

During my (Christy's) childhood, my mother would always read to us from different books. One of the books we would beg her to reread was a book about a busy bee who went to school. The busy bee learned all day long at school, but at the end of the day he learned the most important rule of all, the Golden Rule: Do unto others as you would have others do unto you.

Why should this be any different concerning dating? When you are in a relationship, however "far you go" physically or emotionally is licensing your future husband/wife to do the same. Hold yourself to a higher standard and pray in faith that your future husband/wife will too.

Every night from the time I (Ryan) was a child my parents taught me to pray for my future wife. I continued this until she had a name, Christy. Now I just use that. One of the things I prayed for was that she was being treated with respect and value. You can and should pray this way too. When you pray keep in mind that, *"The effectual, fervent prayer of a righteous man avails much"* (James 5:16).

How do you treat the people you date?

A few questions to ponder…

- Are you taking them for granted? Is that how you'd like to be treated?
- Are you dating this person just to have something to do? That's dishonest.
- Do you emotionally wound them with words – call them names, make fun, criticize, belittle…?
- Do you ever get physical – shove, slap, or hit the other person? Big problems here.
- Guys, do you take advantage of girls sexually?
- Ladies, do you give in sexually, just to feel accepted or desirable?

5. Set Physical boundaries now

"For I am fearfully and wonderfully made"

– Psalm 139:14 NKJ

When speaking to youth across the country I (Ryan) haven't ever been able to get through this section without a few laughs from the crowd. So I welcome yours as well.

Our bodies were created in a magnificent way. God's Word says that we are wonderfully made. When we become aroused sexually, that is part of God's wonderful design. We are designed in such a way that when the arousal comes it is difficult to stop in the middle. It is a process that God designed to be complete and to be fully experienced. When a couple decides to draw the line and wait on sex until marriage, that is great, but the battle is only half won. Carrying out that commitment is a whole different ball game. If you do not choose to draw the line before you get yourselves in a particular sexual situation you will more than likely go "too far." The decision to stop at a particular point is extremely difficult to make in the back seat of a car. If you do not draw the line before sexual arousal begins to occur, you will be fighting against all the forces of nature.

What are some sexual boundaries that Christians should consider? What pleases God? You are the only one who can set your personal limit on how far is "too far". There is a progression leading to sexual intercourse. It begins with a simple touch - holding hands. From there, a hug or embrace then an arm may casually move around a shoulder or waist. Then comes the kissing stage that may include French kissing usually leading to heavy petting. Heavy petting almost always leads to intercourse. So where will you draw your line?

There is a current popular philosophy among young people that says it is not sex if it is only oral sex. Doesn't it stand to reason if an activity involves any sexual organ then it most definitely is sex?

Where you draw the line may be different from your partner's, but each person should respect the other's boundaries. If you are ashamed, uncomfortable, or embarrassed, most likely you have crossed your line and even more important, you've crossed God's. The boundary should be set when you know that after crossing that boundary there is no return. Don't push it!

"For this is the will of God, your sanctification: that you should abstain from sexual immorality"

– I Thessalonians 4:3-5 NKJ

6. Include your family in your dating life

"...The Spirit of God spoke to me and said, [She's the one!]"

– Ryan's mother after first meeting Christy

We cannot stress the importance of this guideline enough. God created the family first. He values family and so should we.

Have you noticed that even the reality television shows like "The Bachelor," and""Meet My Folks," have embraced the importance of family involvement in relationships? Involving your families will benefit you both when you are meeting a family and that family is meeting you.

Your family knows you. They know your likes and dislikes and they can help you discern what is best for you, and they by far have your best interest in mind. I (Christy) can recall numerous times when my younger brother Joe would tell me that certain guys were just not for me. He had my best interest in mind and I could trust him because I knew he was speaking out of love.

Involving your family also allows the person you are in the relationship with the opportunity to see more of who you are. In return you will also learn so much about that person when you get to know their family as well. My (Christy) Aunt Cathy gave me a book about dating when I was first turning my life over to God. It really sparked an interest in finding the right person that God had for me. Allow the people God has given you, family or friends, to be involved into this area of your life.

Some of you reading this may not be close to your family. But we believe that God has placed someone in everyone's life that they can turn to. Maybe it's a friend, a minister, or Grandparents. I (Christy) sometimes sit and wonder where I would be and who I would be if God hadn't placed certain people at certain times in my life. Had my youth ministers, Bill and Melissa not heeded God's voice in coming to my church I wonder who I would have listened to and confided in through my high school years. Look to those that love you. Heed their advice and be grateful for them.

Personal note – Ryan and I met after I first met his parents at a church service. It was *their* idea to bring us together, that's family involvement. Awesome huh?

7. Pray for the purity of your future husband/wife

"Finally brethren, whatever things are true, whatever things are noble, whatever things are just, whatever things are pure, whatever things are lovely, whatever things are of good report, if there is any

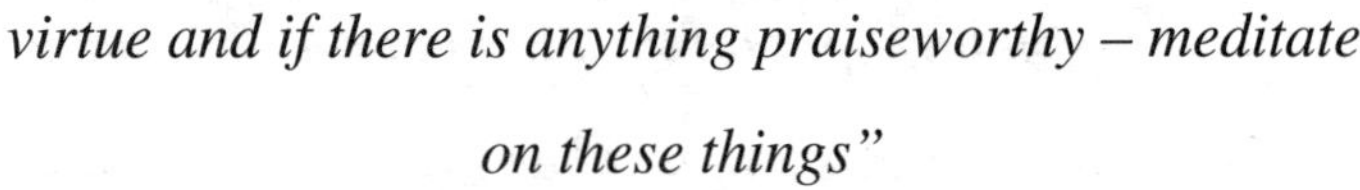

virtue and if there is anything praiseworthy – meditate on these things"

–Philippians 4:8 NKJ

This can revolutionize your dating life. Remember, purity and virginity are not the same. Purity we venture to say is a step above virginity. Purity is maturity. Purity is mental and emotional as well as physical. It is the outcome of delayed gratification of the enjoyment you will share with one special person in marriage.

Do not settle for less. Dating someone who has a foul mouth, vile thoughts, or impure motives only compromises your spiritual standards. Would you marry someone who is clearly unsaved and antagonistic toward God? Then why waste time dating them?

Once you incorporate this principle in your prayer life you will be a more confident person, a less dependant person, and you will begin to grow personally. Pray for the purity of your future mate and begin to see the opposite sex through new eyes, pure eyes.

"...you have put off the old man with his deeds, and have put on the new man who is renewed in knowledge according to the image of Him who created him"

– Colossians 3:9 NKJ

8. Commit to dating Christians only

You cannot expect anyone to love and respect you more than they love and respect their God.

–Ryan and Christy Tate

This principle is discussed in detail in chapter nine, because it is the most important. We need to first get one thing clear: You should never date anyone you could not see yourself marrying.

We hear so many couples say, *"Oh I'm just at a different stage in my life right now," "We're just having fun right now"* or *"We just haven't had 'that' talk yet."* The sad thing about these statements is that they don't realize the damage they are doing to themselves emotionally or physically. Most of them don't understand the concept of "sharing a reputation" with someone.

Ryan wrestled for the University of Oklahoma. The team was Big XII Champions and he also holds several records in the state of California for high school wrestling. He was one of the top recruits in the nation when he graduated from high school. We speak all over the nation to young people and this topic comes up quite a bit. I (Christy) am always asked questions about wrestling, takedowns, double and single legs, but do I know the first thing about it? Not a clue. People assume I know about wrestling because my husband wrestled. Over the last few years I have learned quite a bit more, but still would not enjoy an interview on the subject.

Dating is the same. Whomever you are with, people assume you are the same. You like the same things, enjoy the same things, and yes, believe the same things. Be careful.

Several years ago before my (Ryan) great grandmother died, big family gatherings where held at her farm home in southeastern Oklahoma. On one occasion the family was visiting when we heard loud laughter coming from the back yard. Exiting the house to investigate where the laughter was coming from, we found my great grandmother standing in the back yard by a tree adjacent to her chicken coop. She was laughing at the top of her lungs while throwing her hands back and slapping her knees at the same time. What happened hasn't left me to this day. I constantly remember what happened as a reminder to always follow God's plan for my life, and not settle for the world's cheap imitations.

My great grandmother kept chickens in her back yard for as long as I can remember. Every now and then when the hens weren't laying well she would put a *fake* glass egg in their nests. When the hens would see these eggs they would assume they had already laid them, and since they thought they had done it once, well then why not again. On this particular occasion one of my great grandmother's and her chicken's greatest enemies, the Oklahoma black snake, had crawled into the chicken coop. Once inside, the snake quickly swallowed down what he *believed* was a grade "A" jumbo-sized egg guaranteed to fill you up. It didn't take long for the snake to realize that the egg was not a highly desired afternoon snack but one of my great grandmother's fake glass eggs!

My great grandmother had come across this black snake after it had wrapped itself around a large oak tree in her back yard (snakes often wind around a tree or branch to crack eggs they swallow). This snake had squeezed up against the tree for so long and so hard that it squeezed itself to death trying to crack that glass egg. The laughter came from my great grandmother when she found the old dead snake with the bulge of the fake egg stuck inside.

While the original site was comedic, I later realized that the snake did what you and I are guilty of doing everyday. As we watch television, choose our friends, date, drink, or simply live our lives we are constantly *swallowing down* what our surroundings feed us.

Moral – What we swallow down can destroy us. Be prudent about what you take in. Make sure you're believing and trusting in the genuine Source of spiritual nourishment - not some substitute that may look like the real thing and give temporary pleasure, but in the end be your demise. Be sure you are dating an *authentic* Christian.

The Word of God tells us in 2 Corinthians 6:14 that light cannot have fellowship with darkness. It is because of this reason that you must surround yourself with capable individuals and friends that share your goals and desires in life. We all know the saying, "birds of a feather flock together." This is absolutely the truth. As you make your choices in regards to whom you will date and then someday marry, remember that you become whom you are around. Choose wisely!

"He who walks with wise men will be wise, but the companion of fools will be destroyed."
-Proverbs 13:20 NKJ

9. Date someone who is a spiritual challenge to you

"As iron sharpens iron, so the man sharpens the countenance of his friend."
-Proverbs 27:17 NKJ

About a year or so ago, Christy and I rented the movie "Shallow Hal" starring Gwyneth Paltrow. In the movie, Hal begins to see women's physical appearances based on how they look on the inside. This created some pretty hilarious scenes. We always talk about the movies we see and we joked about how great it would be to be able to see people in that way. After laughing for a while and picturing what certain people would look like we came to realize that we really and truly can see people for how they really are, if we so choose.

The instant I (Ryan) met Christy, my walk with God was deepened. I grew closer to Him and we drew gifts out of each other that glorified God in ways I had never known. We decided that we would marry only if He would be more glorified through our lives together, rather than apart.

"A prudent wife is from the Lord"
– Proverbs 19:14 NKJ

Just being a Christian is not always enough. But it is a good start. Paul talks a lot about baby Christians and their needs. Dating an immature baby Christian can present it's own set of problems. In the natural the needs of a baby are much different than the needs of a teenager or a middle-aged person. It is no different in the spiritual realm. Can you imagine a fifteen year old marrying a 15 month old?

Men need to meet this challenge to be full grown Christian leaders that can lead and be the example Christ intended them to be. When Christy graduated from Oral Roberts University, a Christian University in Tulsa, I (Ryan) found the ratio of men to women staggering – a clear indication that more women than men chose to be at this Christian school. As in many Christian arenas, the women have us beat. Women are begging and praying for us to step up to the plate and be the spiritual leaders in our relationships. Please join me in this effort.

"Husbands love your wives, just as Christ loved the church and gave Himself for her."

– Ephesians 5:25 NKJ

10. Guard your heart

"Keep your heart with all diligence, for out of it springs the issues of life"

—Proverbs 4:23 NKJ

The church does a good job of teaching people to guard their bodies and save themselves for marriage. There are programs like "True Love Waits," and others of that sort. The fact that these programs are impacting people who are choosing to wait until marriage for sex is great. But we believe it is time for the church to take up another banner. Just as important as saving your *body* for marriage is saving your *heart* for marriage.

Women tend to dive into relationships heart first. Some men do as well, but women are more prone. Love is given and emotions are involved from hello. People who do this usually have a pattern of "falling in love" quickly and unfortunately, their heart is broken time and time again. People who give their heart in every relationship do so thinking they are giving their all because this time it just may be the fulfillment of the dream they have had from childhood. In fact, they should have *guarded their heart* until they were absolutely sure.

How do you *guard your heart*? You test the relationship over time. You do not express love until you know the other person feels the same. You don't press for commitment. You take time to *know* the person as a friend. You don't give yourself totally – mind, soul, and body, until you know this is the person God has prepared for you. You *guard your heart* or affections, as an act of discipline until that special someone is revealed.

If you do not master the principle of guarding your heart, you could end up a bitter, hurt or confused person with serious trust issues. One or all of these can carry over into your marriage.

I (Christy) recently interviewed a cardiologist on a local television station here in Oklahoma. We discussed a friend of mine who recently had bypass surgery. The doctor proceeded to tell me even the slightest change in heart rhythm can affect a person dramatically. If your heart were to stop pumping blood into one area it could result in serious damage to parts of the body or even death. Imagine now taking your heart and passing it around a room filled with people you have dated in the past. These are people you gave your heart. Are they holding it lightly? Do they gladly receive it? Do they treat it with gentleness and care? Do they know how to handle it? Are they mishandling it - dropping it on the floor and leaving it? Are they stepping on it, even stomping on it?

Janis Joplin sang, "Take another little piece of my heart."[2] Has that happened to you? You've given your heart a piece at a time to several. Visualize yourself today retrieving your heart, even if it's in pieces, then taking it directly and to the Healer, Jehovah Rapha (Greek for healer). Leave your heart in the hands of Jesus until He sees fit to entrust it to the one person He has prepared and created to hold your heart.

Guard your heart. It is your lifeline to a successful marriage.

Reading these ten guidelines for dating is an excellent start down the path of meeting your future husband/wife. However, they are simply words on a page until you get them off the page and into your life and heart.

In addition, read the book of Ruth. It's short (only four chapters). It is a beautiful love story based on honoring God's commands when you are in love with someone. Men, do not settle on a woman if she is not a Ruth. Proverbs says that a man is blessed when he finds a wife, not just any woman, there is a difference. Women, make sure he is a Boaz before even offering your heart. Studies show that most people picture God in a way that resembles their natural fathers. Remember ladies, you are choosing the father of your children and the children *will* determine what God is like by his fatherly example. This is not to be taken lightly.

Marriage always begins with a date.

– Ryan and Christy Tate

CHAPTER FOUR

Somewhere Out There...

The Search

Somewhere Out There...

The Search

"For the vision is yet for an appointed time, but at the end it shall speak, and not lie: though it tarry, wait for it; because it will surely come, it will not tarry."
-Habakkuk 2:3 NKJ

Faith is believing in advance what will only make sense in reverse.
-Jo Ann Levell

When my (Christy) brother Joe joined the Marine Corp, he was chosen during SOI (School of Infantry) to be in a program called Yankee White. Less than one percent of Marines are chosen for this very prestigious position. Our family was very proud of him, but not surprised. The reason few Marines are chosen is because they must be investigated thoroughly. Their past, their friends, and family were all put under a microscope. I was the only one home when a federal agent pulled up in a white sedan asking questions about my brother's reputation. This detailed process had to happen because he was going to be required to carry a loaded weapon in the presence of the most powerful man in the nation, the President of the United States. Joe passed with flying colors and served as a guard for the Clinton and Bush administrations at Camp David.

Likewise when dating, you are in essence screening or investigating another person. If you are not doing that now, you should be. The position you are attempting to fill is even more important than who is chosen to guard the President. This person will be guarding your children, your dreams, your goals, your life, and your soul. Our process of selection should not be any less detailed and it should be mandatory.

Scripture says that *"In the beginning…was God."* The Bible also states that God is Love. He is not about love, or interested in love, it says He IS Love. So, if God is love and you are looking for love then you better get smart and put God at the CENTER of your search for love.

There is a popular country-western song which says, "Lookin' for love in all the wrong places, lookin' for love in all the wrong faces…" Maybe part of the problem with your search is found in the words of that song. Start your search first in your relationship with God and then remember that God orders the steps of the righteous. Remember, your search will always begin where you are in your life. If you are not right with God, your search will not be right with Him either, and you probably won't enjoy the results. If you are a woman, one of the most important principles to acknowledge is that Proverbs says you are a treasure to your husband, and the treasure does not do the looking…a treasure is discovered!

When I (Ryan) was a teenager our family lived in Southern California. We went to a beautiful flower nursery on the Pacific coast near Carlsbad, California one weekend. There were acres and acres of beautiful flowers of every color of the rainbow. As I walked through the flowers I saw a beautiful butterfly flitting from blossom to blossom. I decided that butterfly was no match for my youthful speed and proceeded to chase it down. To my shock and amazement I could not even get close. As soon as I was near enough to grab it, it would sail off out of reach. In total defeat (not my style as a ten year old!) I gave up and sat down among the flowers. I had been there for only a minute or so watching the ocean in the distance and enjoying the beautiful scenery when I sensed a presence near my shoulder. My sister Trinity, standing a few yards away shouted in glee at me, “Ryan,” she called, “Don’t move, the butterfly has landed on your shoulder!” Indeed, there sat the elusive creature next to my ear quietly moving its wings up and down. When I stopped working so hard and came to a place of rest, the butterfly decided to join me. I still have the photograph my sister took of the multicolored creature sitting on the bill of my baseball cap!

Maybe you have tried to work too hard in the search. When you find a place of stillness in who you are in Christ, then the Savior of the world and Lord of the universe has a chance to work on your behalf. Stop working so hard and start trusting more in His ability to bring the right person into your life. Remember, a real key to finding the right kind of person and that person being able to find you is to be in the right places. If you search in a bar you will find prospects that are the opposite of what you desire. Find the right field then sit down and trust in God’s hand and leadership.

Thank well when she comes to you, the woman who understands.

–Everard Jack Appleton,

The Woman Who Understands

When Ryan and I first began to date some years ago he captured my heart with an email he sent to me one August. His words were exactly what I needed to hear and wanted to hear. I had found that young men were in such a hurry to get on with a relationship that they left out the most important part of the search. Ryan's email holds a special page in my scrapbook. He wrote, "*...I am looking forward to seeing you and pursuing a friendship. You are right when you say that God reveals Himself when you least expect it. I believe God opens some doors while He shuts others, and it is up to us to seek His desires and have patience enough to wait and walk through the doors He opens and forget about the one He has closed.*"

If your search is to find a person who can join you in seeking God, you are on the right track. Run from anything else.

One key to remember in the search, are you *steering* or *drifting*? Don't allow yourself to drift along in the search. When ships are lost at sea the U.S. Coast Guard begins a search effort.[3] They do not just drift along hoping to bump into the lost vessel. They have a specific plan of action, with sightings, as well as latitude and longitude coordinates. They follow that plan, and are successful most of the time because of the plan.

Every person needs love and affection. Sadly, many people enter marriage without the confidence that they have married the right person. In fact, more than 90 percent of all the people in the United States will marry at least once during their lifetime. But each year in the Unites States, more that 200,000 marriages end prior to the couples' second anniversary.

Why do some end their search with such a sad result? Our society teaches individuals to rely almost totally on their instincts when choosing a mate. When it comes to a good wise choice in your search for the "right one" you need to examine these critical factors. Here are some traps to avoid as you search.

- Deciding too quickly
- Deciding too young
- Over eagerness
- Choosing a mate to please someone else
- Not enough experience base
- Unrealistic Expectations [4]

Do you feel as though you've dated bits and pieces of your ideal mate? Like the scientist in Frankenstein, you've wanted to put together all of the good qualities of former boyfriends or girlfriends. "I'd give her Jill's sense of humor, Marissa's eyes, Ashley's honesty, and Kate's income." Or are you unsure of what exactly you want? "I'll know Mr. Right when I see him." One hundred boyfriends later, you're still searching. In casual dating relationships, people tend focus on finding someone who will make them laugh, who is fun to be with and/or highly physically attractive. While these characteristics are important, they are not an adequate foundation for building a life together. Compatible goals for life, financial perspectives, spiritual outlooks, and emotional maturity are essential in maintaining a committed, lifelong relationship. No one is perfect and you can't expect to change someone, just as you would not want him or her to change you.

How can you know if someone is right for you for the long haul? A good way to begin is by evaluating five general areas of compatibility: emotional, spiritual, intellectual, physical, and financial. Objectively and honestly assess yourself in these areas, as well as what you expect or desire from a future spouse. This excerpt from a letter written to me (Christy) by Ryan before we were married says it best.

Dearest Christy,

I am beside you right now. I feel as if I have been here my whole life. Ever since we met we have talked about how God brought us together and how amazing everything is. I can't even begin to explain how unbelievable you are and how blessed I am to have you. My entire day starts and ends with you. I have a better relationship with God, and I Ryan Tate, "Mr. Accomplishment," have more drive to succeed and provide than ever before in my life. This is all because of you. I don't even remember a time when I was without you. I will make it my life's goal to love you the way you deserve to be loved. I will love you spiritually, mentally, emotionally, and physically.

SPIRITUALLY

Christy you are the definition of a good Christian. God is apparent every time I look upon you. It is much easier to love God because of you. I always knew that the woman I would marry had to be a Christian and love God. I never imagined she could be as amazing as you. You are the type of person that people dream about becoming, yet you are not arrogant, conceded, or egocentric. You always give God the glory, and that is why He blesses you. With the world as crazy as it is, it is so easy for individuals to use their talents and abilities solely for personal gain. Not you, Christy the way you are with people and your ability to use your gifts to reach out to others and spread God's Word is one of the most attractive qualities you have. I will always nurture and support this in you, as you will in me. I will lead us to always be godly and Christ centered. You have my word. Thank you for your love of God and your life. It is what makes you who you are, and I will never accept anything else other than total devotion to Him.

MENTALLY

You are one of the smartest women I have ever met. Scratch that, you are one of the smartest women the world has ever seen. You have wisdom unparalleled for your age, and insight into people I have never seen. Once again these are all qualities that had to be present for me. Intellectually you are one of the most stimulating people I have ever known. You are just plain smart. You are an independent thinker and use common sense better than anyone. You are open to other opinions and can enter into any conversation without hesitation. I love your mind; it is another one of your extremely attractive qualities. I will always listen to you and heed your opinions. I already know that if I will listen to your advice and counsel we will be not only the most successful individuals in the world, but more importantly the happiest.

EMOTIONALLY

I promise to be by your side through everything. Whether it is good or bad, happy or sad, there will always be one thing you can count on: me right beside you. Christy, I promise to cherish your emotions and feelings. Your love for me is the greatest gift I have ever received other than my salvation and

I will always remember that. I always want you to look at me and feel safe and secure. I want to be the definition of strength, reliability, and honesty in your eyes. You are so dear to me, and to be there for you is a dream come true. As a woman you are more emotional than a man and I love that about you. Christy you wear your heart on your sleeve. I love your openness with me and trust. To know that you believe in me empowers me to achieve against all odds. I thank you for that. I will always protect and provide for you and be consistent for you.

PHYSICALLY

You have been blessed with one of the most amazingly perfect figures this world has ever seen. Simply touching your skin or smelling your hair gives me more pleasure than you'll ever know. Holding you near and caressing your body is a blessing that I can't even put into words. Everything around me can be crazy and out of control, but when I hold you in my arms or place my nose down the line of your neck all is well. Every touch, glance, or whisper is a first time. You are a continual surprise of wonderful qualities that make you the most amazing partner in the world. To share my life with you will be a wonderful world of love and affection. Do you know that simply by taking my hand, or kissing my cheek while whispering, "I love you" in my ear makes me the happiest man in the world? I will share you with no one and desire no one else. You are my dream and I want nothing but you. My whole life I have looked for something better. Now I can honestly say that I have found the best. You are the most beautiful and desirable women I have ever laid eyes on. Such a blessing does not happen to everyone and I will gladly accept it. I can't thank you enough.

I know that I have carried on for way too long with this, but sometimes I want you to just know how I feel. I am in a constant state of euphoria because of you. I am so grateful that you have chosen me to love. I will never take this lightly. It is the single most important worldly thing I could have. Thank you. Always tell me the desires of your heart and never have any fears about what I will say to any of your concerns or questions. I will always put you first. Remember, don't ever let me stop making you feel special. You don't deserve anything else. You are perfect for me.

Love always and forever, Ryan

CHAPTER FIVE

Takin' Care Of Business...

Rules of Relationships

Takin' Care Of Business...

Rules of Relationships

"In honor, preferring one another."
-Romans 12:10 KJV

Guard your tongue when your husband is angry.
-St. Monica

Pamela Paul's new book The Starter Marriage and The Future of Matrimony, talks about generation Xers (born between 1965 and 1978) who may be in love with the idea of marriage but don't have a clue how to make marriage successful.[5] According to Paul's book, spending by generations X-ers on the wedding day has leaped nearly 20 percent in the last five years, but they're also splitting up faster than couples before them. Nearly one in ten 25-34 year olds who have been married are now divorced, a 40 percent increase from 1970. Today's young adults haven't a clue about how to make a marriage work. "We live in a matrimonial mania culture," she says. "There's a lot of focus on the wedding day, but we give little thought to the 50 years that follow." One important factor, says Paul, is that so many generation Xers are children of divorce and lack models of lasting marriages. Many women accept the first marriage proposal because they are afraid another offer might not come along.[6]

We urge you who are considering marriage to forget focusing on the perfect dress or reception and ask yourself some tough questions. Take a closer look at marriages that fail and those that succeed. What are the differences? Stop expecting that marriage will be the cure-all, the one ticket to everlasting happiness.

Every couple marrying today is at risk. After they toss the bouquet and return the tuxedos, couples often assume they're headed for marital bliss. Statistics of couples who recently tied the knot reveal that 4% already reported having *serious* marital problems. Half were already having doubts about whether their marriages would last.[7] How sad. Most engaged couples prepare more for their wedding than they do for their marriage. The $20 billion-a-year wedding industry can testify to that fact.[8] People are just not taking the marriage steps seriously – there is no accountability.

When I (Ryan) ran for State Representative there were many rules to follow concerning the money spent on the campaign and campaign donations. Over $10,000 dollars was spent on the campaign and we had to account for every cent by turning the records over to the Oklahoma Ethics Commission. In the same way, relationships should have rules and accountability too if we want them to run smoothly (especially in marriage) and succeed. God is holding you accountable.

NEEDS – WE GOT EM
(Understanding His Needs/Her Needs)

To say that men and women are different is the most understated thing we could tell you in this book. Christy and I rejoiced when we were able to get an automobile with dual temperature controls. That meant that we wouldn't constantly be having to compromise on the setting – she was continually cold in the car and I was always turning the heat down. We discovered early in marriage that we are so different that we even have–*totally* different needs. A "need" is something that is necessary for one's own personal health or well-being. Remember a need is not something he or she would *like* to have, a need is something they *must* have – essential things. For a deeper look into the needs of men and women we recommend the Bible study workbook, 11 Reasons Families Succeed, also offered by Family Solutions.[9] If you are engaged or thinking of starting a family we would encourage you to get the workbook and complete it together.

Before we talk about those different needs note the following:

NEEDS VS. NEEDY – BIG DIFFERENCE!

Here's the deal. Normal healthy people have specific needs that we are going to discuss in a moment. The object of dating and marriage is to learn how to meet those needs. However if you are dating or involved with a *needy* person – good luck! Quite frankly you will never be able to meet their needs. You know this type – they are never satisfied – you simply can't do enough to make them happy. The more you give, the more they want. To even seriously date such an individual is setting oneself up for constant failure because nothing is ever enough! The *needy* person is a candidate for serious counseling, even professional help. If prayer and intense therapy produce a definite and lasting change in the individual, then and only then should you consider marrying a *needy* person.

SHE IS LOOKING FOR SOMEONE WHO WILL MEET HER NEEDS

#1

She Needs To Feel Important and Valued

A woman needs to believe that she is the most precious priority of a man's life. She needs to feel valuable, and treasured. The young man who knows how to treat a young lady with preciousness will be the one who treasures her. Don't you take good care of something you consider valuable? Women sense quickly the place they hold in a man's life. She knows when his sports interest, his hobby, his other friends, even his job is more important than her. It is sad to see a woman who does not feel valued in a relationship– she feels used and most often is constantly competing for his attention. You can recognize her usually because she will have low self-esteem and could even suffer with depression. But the woman who feels most valued and precious, she flourishes in that lofty, loving position.

#2

She Needs the Truth

Have you seen the bumper sticker that reads "BOYS LIE?"[10] It is usually attached to a teenaged girls car. How sad is it that too many young women today are already convinced that this is true of most men. Women need honesty because they need to trust a man's words and his motives, for her own safety and well-being. She has the highest respect for the man who will "be absolutely truthful" even when it hurts. Some men believe that they have to "shield" or "protect" the woman from the truth. Nothing could be farther out of line. What really hurts her is to find out the truth from someone else, or discover the truth for herself later and feel deceived. She also needs honesty about the relationship. Men, don't feign love for her, if all you really want is sex. Don't lead her on because you don't have the courage to be honest about your feelings. That is lying and lying does more damage than the truth ever could.

#3

She Needs Someone Financially Stable

Of course, in a dating relationship this aspect is not as important as it will be in marriage. But even in serious dating relationships a woman needs to sense that the man is financially responsible and that he wants to provide security, peace, and protection for those he loves. If the man gives off vibes that he would rather not work, if he is basically lazy and doesn't hold down a job those are bright red flags - be cautious. The lack of financial stability produces great anxiety for a woman. Notice that we are not saying the woman needs a rich man with lots and lots of money. She doesn't need wealth, designer clothes, or a new car from her boyfriend. What she *does* need is the feeling of safety that comes when she knows he will help to meet her basic needs and the needs of her children one day. She has the highest regard for a man

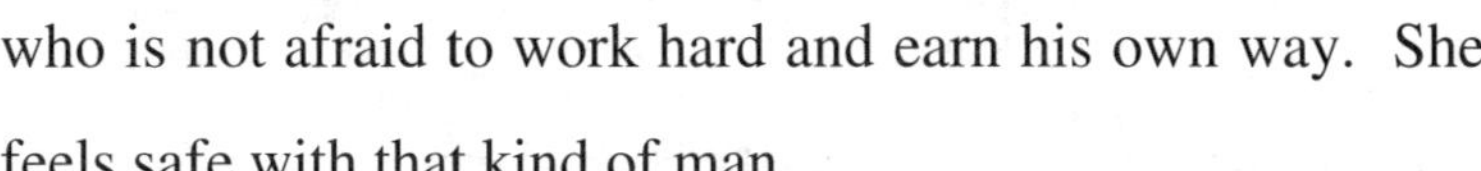

who is not afraid to work hard and earn his own way. She feels safe with that kind of man.

#4

She Needs a Family Man

A woman in a healthy dating relationship will be able to determine if the man will make a good father and be committed to the family she hopes to have. Usually she can tell by how he treats his own family – his parents or his siblings. Does he value "family" traditions and does he make time for family? Women appreciate and respect a man who demonstrates to her that he will be committed to his family first. Have you observed marriages where the man makes time for everything else but his family? His family seems to be left out of his life entirely. Some men are apparently more committed to their jobs, their sports interest or hobby. A woman needs a man she knows will give his time and his interest first of all to his family. It is incredibly important that children believe that they are important and that "daddy" makes time to be with them, listen to them, and be involved in every part of their lives.

#5

She Needs A Man Who Is Teachable.

Let us explain this one. Put another way, a woman needs a man who is willing to learn, to change and to grow. She needs a man who isn't always right? Believe it or not guys, you can be wrong! Manly men are so intimidated and threatened that they cannot admit when they have been wrong, they seldom say they are sorry, and hardly ever ask for forgiveness. Real men are teachable – they are willing to change when they see the error of their ways.

Women feel safe with a man who can also learn from her. He sees things that she can teach him that would make him a better man. He receives her insight, her emotional strength, her intellect and sees how they would be an advantage to him.

Lastly, this man also will be spiritually teachable. A woman needs a man who will be open to listening and following God's direction and change accordingly. The strongest men we know are those who are willing to say, *"I'm sorry," "I was wrong,"* and *"Will you forgive me?"*

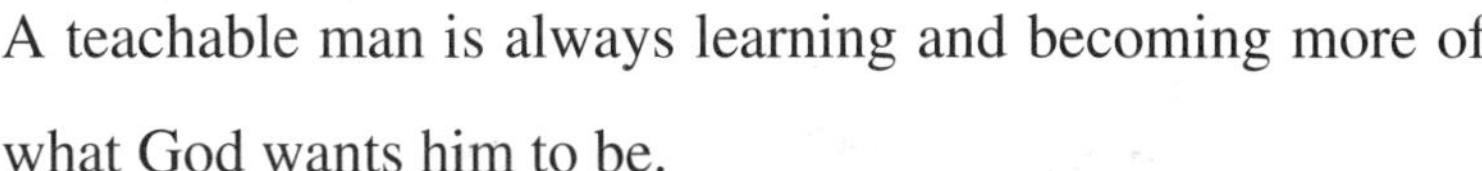

A teachable man is always learning and becoming more of what God wants him to be.

#6

She Needs A Man Who Will Talk

Yes it's true; women are more verbal than men.[11] Sometimes women are accused of being too talkative, nosy, or obtrusive when actually they are only demonstrating their need for information. A woman feels safe when she knows the details. The only way she can get the information she needs is to hear the "words." She appreciates a man's attempt to meet her need for information and conversation. Some of the saddest women are those who do not have anyone to talk to – their husbands will not meet this need. A woman needs words not only of *information*, but she also needs words of *affirmation*. She needs to be told how you feel about her, why you love her, and why she is special to you. A man who meets a woman's need for words demonstrates that she is valuable enough to be listened to, and her spoken thoughts are appreciated.

#7

She Needs a Spiritual Leader

Every woman needs a man to be the spiritual leader God created him to be. She prays for that kind of man. Of course, many men just refuse to be the spiritual leader or have rejected Christ altogether. Sometimes women find themselves forced into the leadership position in a relationship or marriage, but that is not God's perfect plan. A woman needs a man who will lead out in prayer, in learning and obeying the Word of God. She looks to the future and needs a man who will be the godly example for her and her children. Even in dating situations she is looking for the man who will lead her spiritually.

Now the guys turn…

He Is Looking For Someone Who Will Meet His Needs

#1

He Needs To Be Admired

This one is easy to observe. From little boys to grown men it is apparent that males thrive on admiration. Wise indeed is the woman who has learned to find those things that she can admire in a man and verbalize that admiration. That is the way most men *feel* loved. Now, to be even more specific – he needs *your* admiration. More than anyone else, he feels strong, capable, and hopeful when he has the admiration of the woman he loves and values. Everyone else around him may not be meeting this need, in fact, they may be criticizing him or berating him, but if he has one special woman's admiration – he can go on, he has purpose, and he has hope. He may be in a job or circumstance where he has little outside praise or affirmation; he needs the woman's words or actions that say, *"I believe in you, I admire you for (whatever…)."*

Try this on your man – he will seemingly change right before your eyes. That man will feel successful and fulfilled.

#2

He Needs A Woman Who Understands His Sexual Needs

Sexual needs, such as physical intimacy and sexual intercourse are to be fulfilled only in a loving marriage relationship. However, it will be important in a serious dating relationship that the woman understands the male's need for sexual fulfillment. Let us be clear, here. This is a legitimate male need. God created men to be sexual by nature in ways women may find difficult to understand. For example, a man is more easily stimulated sexually by visual images. A casual touch does more physically to men. One major difference is that the physical release from orgasm is one of the most powerful, physical urges for the man. Women may misunderstand the male's sexual drive and accuse him of being *too* pre-occupied with sex, even over-sexed. She may attempt to make the man feel guilty or suggest something is wrong with him. When a woman realizes sexual fulfillment is a man's *need* she will be open and even feel honored to be the one in the future who will meet that need. However, if he is pressuring you for sex before marriage, if he uses pornography, or if he verbalizes sexual fantasies that include bondage or the degradation of women – there *is* something wrong. A Christian man puts his sexual needs on hold for marriage, protects the one he loves by waiting, and acknowledges that it is difficult but that she is worth the wait.

#3

He Needs Peace In A Troubled World

A man needs to feel in control of some part of his life. He needs a place of shelter, a harbor, a respite from the chaotic world. Ideally that place will be his home and his future wife will have a great deal of responsibility in helping him to create such a place. To return home after a days work at a stressful job to a safe, loving, and happy home will make the difference for him emotionally, physically, and even spiritually. Notice we are not saying that he needs a place free from conflict or stress. Sometimes, events are stressful in the home and at times, there will be conflict. But, he needs to know that the woman he loves will help establish a sense of normalcy in a place where things are the way they are supposed to be. Today many women/wives work outside the home too and we are not suggesting it is the woman's responsibility alone to create a peaceful home for the man regardless of what he does. It is important for a woman to understand the man's need for a place of order and peace.

#4

He Needs a Beautiful Woman

Whoa! You say, Ryan and Christy, you have blown it here. The feminists will be all over this one. So, as a disclaimer let us say, that beauty is relative isn't it? What one man says is beautiful, another might reject. The important thing is to realize that a man needs a woman that *he* is proud of. As the old saying goes, "there is no accounting for taste." We are not saying a man needs a woman with a perfect figure or the most beautiful face according to the latest "Cosmopolitan" issue. But, a man *does* need a woman who strives to be as attractive as *she* can be. In our society appearance is way too important, however, it remains true that often the first impression lands the job, opens the door, or makes the sale. In that context, a wife will be an extension of her husband, his tastes, his leadership, his values, and his priorities. So, a man needs a woman who is personally attractive, confidant, and content. By the way, the Christian woman has a built in beauty already at her disposal – a beautiful spirit, a gentle voice, and a welcoming smile that is evidence of the Holy Spirit dwelling within. Now – *that* is a beautiful woman!

#5

A Man Needs A Personal Cheerleader

What do we mean? Every man needs one person, ideally the woman he loves, to be his greatest cheerleader. You know what a cheerleader does - she supports the team, believes in the team, and celebrates the team whether the team wins or loses. Well, you say, isn't that covered in the man's need for admiration? Not really. You see, a man needs admiration, but he also needs someone who stands with him when he hasn't done anything for which he deserves admiration. He needs someone who supports him even when he has really messed up, or when he has had the worst day of his life. How encouraging it will be to the man who finds a woman who will be there for him when everyone else has given up on him.

I (Ryan) watched my sister Trinity through out our high school and college days as she cheered on the sidelines. Even when the team was losing, through good games or blowouts, Trinity demonstrated faithful support and encouragement – that is what cheerleaders do. That is exactly what a man is looking for and needing in a woman— a cheerleader, someone who believes in him even when he is having trouble believing in himself.

#6

He Needs a Woman With a Sweet, Gentle Spirit

A godly man is looking for a woman with a sweet, sensitive, and gentle spirit. It probably would be easier explained if we looked at a woman who is the opposite. Do you know the kind of woman who is constantly complaining, whining, and negative? Imagine living with that woman. Forget it! He needs a woman who is positive, loving, and flexible. Why? Because he is looking for a woman who will be a partner with him as he provides warmth, understanding, and guidance to his children. A woman who is easily offended, angry most of the time, vindictive and judgmental will not be able to guide and direct children in a positive way.

If a woman is constantly given to mood swings or childish temper tantrums, she will create fear in a home, not security. The vulgar, bitter or angry spirited woman is not a candidate for any serious relationship, much less marriage.

#7

He Needs A Woman's Gift of Intuition

No, this is not an attempt to validate something that some call "imaginary." Women really *do* have intuitive gifts that men do not possess. We call it "radar" in our house. Christy may feel or sense something about someone or some event and express it to me. I have a choice – I can either reject it as silly over reaction, *or* I can trust my wife's intuitive gift and heed her words and feelings to help me proceed with that person or event. When a man is willing to be influenced by a woman's intuitive gifts *he* will be the one to benefit. Women are usually more discerning of people's motives. (Remember Pilate's wife in Matt. 27:19 – she tried to warn her husband about Jesus – if only he had listened!) By the way, women are more likely to read another *woman's* motives, or catch hints of deception that may escape her male counterpart. Can these "radar" signals be wrong? Yes, but amazingly, they are more often right on! Women also quickly catch on to people who use deceptive or misleading words. A man needs his wife's "radar" or intuition just because her feelings and thoughts are valuable to him. He doesn't have to "obey" her and always agree with her intuition, but the wise man listens out of love and appreciation for this very real feminine gift.

As you can see, the needs of men and women can be very different. It is important to understand that the only way to truly succeed at any relationship is to attempt to meet your partner's needs to the best of your ability. Thank God for enabling you, and enjoy the results of following the rules of relationships.

CHAPTER SIX

Everybody Was Kung-Fu Fighting...

Handling Conflict and Baggage

Everybody Was Kung-Fu Fighting...

Handling Conflict and Baggage

"He that is slow to anger is better than the mighty; and he that rules his spirit than he that takes a city."

-Proverbs 16:32 NKJ

If two people agree about everything all of the time, one of them is not necessary.
-Ryan Tate

The engagement can be one of the happiest, yet one of the toughest periods of time for a couple. For that reason, we would definitely recommend a short engagement period. Once you become engaged (which many readers may be) you don't really have any defined roles. You aren't the boyfriend or the girlfriend anymore, and you aren't the husband or the wife either. You are in a sort of twilight zone. You aren't married, but you feel the responsibility of sharing a life with one another, and you can't sleep together yet (sexual impulses are greater because you now know this is the person you will be with for the rest of your life). So if you are anything like us, you will find this to be a trying time. Even your conflict may escalate due to this sometimes stressful period.

We believe that one of the biggest reasons for conflict during dating, engagement, and early in marriage happens when couples are trying to define personal rules. Human nature tells us that we must be strong and not be pushed around. We think we shouldn't put up with too much from our partner or they might take advantage and always expect us to back down. We push the lines and test each other's faithfulness and commitment. Plain and simple, this behavior is acting out of fear, the exact *opposite* of acting out of love.

All conflict, not just during the time of engagement and dating, stems from fear. We fear rejection so *we* reject. We fear abandonment, so *we* walk out before we have the chance of being hurt. We fear pain, so we put *ourselves* in positions to administer it, so pain can't touch us. Don't try to condition the person by building up walls of defense before an attack is even launched. Human nature will always try to beat the other to the punch. True love cannot survive in this environment. It doesn't even have any room to grow and is definitely not nourished. Our nature must be changed'– born again. Be free from fear by taking a chance with love. Love sent Jesus to die on the cross and He gave us an option of choosing Him or not. Let us follow His lead. Believe in love.

"There is no fear in love; but perfect love casts out fear, because fear involves torment. But he who fears has not been made perfect in love."

-I John 4:18 NKJ

We do not believe that any couple sets out to have a marriage filled with fussing and fighting. However, make no mistake, if you are normal you will argue and have disagreements. Ryan always says that if two people agree about everything all of the time, one of them is not necessary. As we stated in an earlier chapter, when you marry you not only keep *your* daily ups and downs, but you inherit a whole extra set of someone else's problems. No one sets out to have a marriage full of conflict. Then why do so many relationships fall apart because of conflict? Something must be wrong.

Reading this book puts you ahead of the game. Problems are easier to avoid if they haven't occurred yet, so these are things you can watch for and beware of while considering marriage. If you ignore these potential problems and do not talk about them before you marry, you will more than likely end up living them out. We don't know about you, but we would choose the former.

We've determined that conflict is a normal part of relationships. It is how we handle conflict that is most important. There can be a multitude of reasons for conflict, however we believe that it boils down to five basic "lovebusters", things couples do in a relationship that breaks down the love. As you read about these five lovebusters, *stop and consider* whether or not you are contributing to any of them in your relationship now.[12] Then, *stop and consider* if your current boyfriend or girlfriend is contributing to them now. If either of you are, it WILL continue into your marriage if not eliminated prior to it.

Lovebuster #1

ANNOYING BEHAVIOR -

Early one morning I (Christy) remember getting up to catch a flight and grabbing a quick bowl of cereal from the kitchen before I had to get ready. As I was eating I heard a loud voice coming from the bedroom, "I can hear you crunching from in here!", followed by laughter that was just as loud. How embarrassing! But even more so, how annoying! All of the years I had made fun of my dad for crunching his food, and my new husband is now making fun of me (funny how things work that way).

This is one funny example of annoying behavior, but there can be many others, and deeper annoyances as well. Some can even be detrimental to relationships. They can hurt feelings, cause pain and depression, and even leave scars. Most of us have at least one annoying behavior trait and have had them long before we entered a relationship. However, they must be dealt with while in the early stages of your relationship before they do major damage. Let's take a look at some examples of annoying behavior.

- *Ignoring your partner* – This can destroy a relationship. Review the chapter on rules of relationships. Women especially have a need for conversation.

- *Being Moody* – Being moody can drain your relationship faster than almost anything. We must be in control of our moods and realize that God has given us power over them.
- *Complaining* – Have you ever asked someone how they are doing and wished you hadn't asked? Don't be a negative person. It breeds a spirit that brings people down and others can sense it when they walk in the door. Run from this pattern of behavior, it can kill your joy.
- *Pride* – Instead of marrying a prideful person, why don't you run your head into a brick wall about 50 million times? This type of person is always right, and I mean always. Biting through steel would be easier than getting them to apologize. Proverbs tells us that pride comes before destruction, so if you are in a relationship with a prideful person you can look forward to a destructive marriage.
- *Jealousy* – The Word of God is very clear on envy and jealousy. It refers to them as *"rottenness in a person's bones"*, and that *"no one can stand"* before

them. In other words, jealousy can kill a relationship. In the natural, it makes the jealous person very unattractive to their mate. Jealousy defies a core pillar of successful relationships: trust. Learn to love yourself and trust your mate. This will lead you off of the road of jealousy.

- *Shop-aholic* – This must be under control before you begin a marriage and especially before you start a family. Read chapter eight on finances. Ryan and I never make significant purchases without first consulting each other. Be respectful and grateful. Prioritize together and be considerate.

There are many other annoyances that can hurt a relationship. Talk about your weaknesses and discuss the habits you have. Get to know the person before you marry and you can avoid many of these problems. Things will always come up and everyone has their own little pet peeves, but listen to each other. Allow each other to express feelings, then practice mercy and self-control.

Lovebuster #2

DISRESPECT –

I (Christy) asked my Grandma Fredda (who has been married to my Grandpa over 50 years) what the key was to a happy marriage, she replied without hesitation,"Respect." How true. We have asked many couples what one thing they would change, and so often the answer is in the area of respect. Aretha Franklin sure hit home with that famous line, "All I'm askin' is for a little R-E-S-P-E-C-T."

Some of the best advice given to me was from my (Christy) youth minister's wife Melissa, just before Ryan and I married. She said, "Christy, do not respect him any less in his weaknesses." Respect is honoring and preferring one another. It is regarding that person as worthy of kindness and sincerity. Get into a marriage with a disrespectful person and kiss your personal self-esteem and confidence good-bye.

People disrespect their partner for many reasons. However, disrespect is often times given in retaliation from disrespect received from the other person. It may be one of the most difficult verses in the Bible to apply, but I Peter 3:9 tells us not to return an evil for an evil, but the contrary; a *blessing* for evil. Wow! How hard is that? It's just like everything else - it comes easier with practice.

A good "respect" test for your boyfriend or girlfriend is simple. *Observe the way he treats his mother and how she treats her father.* You will more than likely be plugged right into that same respect outlet and be treated similarly over time.

Lovebuster #3

DEMANDS

If any of these lovebusters are characterized by fear, this is the one. Demanding people feel they must control every situation, or things will fall into shambles around them. Demands are made out of fear that if asked, the person would not willingly give. Sadly enough many times this is true. If two demanding people marry, the relationship is a constant fight for position. Love often dies amid impossible demands and threats. Prevent this at all costs. Learn to communicate and listen to each other. The most devestating thing about demanding people is that they are not free to experience the love others have to offer. They are too busy controlling the way they want love to be shown or spoken. Sad case.

A good way *not* to end up here is to learn how to communicate. If we could sum communication up in one word it would be this: LISTEN. We mean really listen. Don't listen only to respond or to react – listen to *understand.* We tend to only listen with our ears, try listening with your heart. You may hear something they've been trying to tell you for a long time.

Lovebuster #4

DISHONESTY

Nothing kills love faster than dishonesty. When a person is dishonest you can count on that person not being very close to you. You will not know them emotionally, mentally, or spiritually because you don't trust them. They are living a lie and many times in turn you will be also. If the person you are with has a problem with the truth, run! Satan is the father of lies and if your boyfriend or girlfriend does not get a grip and take control in this area, the lying will overtake them and eventually they will become a chronic liar (see the needs section in the previous chapter – honesty is a basic need).

Dishonesty leads to distrust, and trust is the foundation for a successful relationship. Kick out trust and you've lost the foundation to your whole building. Be wise and discerning. Don't be suspicious, be discerning (there is a difference). God does not cut any slack in this area. And I quote the psalmist,' *"I hate and abhor lying..."*(Psalm 119:163).

Lovebuster #5

ABUSE

If you are in a relationship with an abusive person (verbal or physical) we would advise you to get out now. Don't wait for change or try to be a fixer. You can pray for them, but God wants to get you out of the way so He can first do some work on them. The abuser is probably not a believer and will not have the conviction of the Holy Spirit inside of him or her that would give them any desire to stop. Ephesians chapter four tells us that we are to put off the old man and to put on the new. Nothing in or about abuse has anything to do with the new man, which we are commanded to "put on."

Marriage will not fix the abuse problem. Please do not buy into this lie from satan that says, "after we marry he/she will calm down and change, they will not be as abusive." It will only get worse and you will be let down. Don't walk away, don't even run, zoom out of this type of relationship.

We ask that you take this chapter very seriously. Take a long hard look at these five lovebusters. Do you fall under the category of a lovebuster? If so, moving on to a new relationship will not fix the problem, it will only follow you. You will continue the pattern if you don't recognize it and determine to change. If it is your partner who demonstrates the lovebusters, realize the limits they are placing on love and don't stand for it. Do not wait for them to change – be honest and tell them why you are moving on. Many of these lovebusters are carried from one relationship to another. They must be dealt with and destroyed before you can ever have a successful relationship.

You might have read through the section on lovebusters and thought, "That's great Ryan and Christy, but what do I do if my partner is okay now, then changes later?" Good question. Usually people are like onions. The closer you get and the more layers they reveal, the smellier they become. This takes time and we usually don't sell the worst side of ourselves to anyone. That side is called BAGGAGE.

CHECK BAGS HERE!

Baggage is something that every person has, and can show itself in many forms. People can have bags full of neglect, low self-esteem, distrust, selfishness, no conflict resolution skills, life perception, and so many more. Regardless of what they are, the day you come home from the honeymoon people usually unpack many more bags than expected.

Your future mate has been with his or her family for quite a long time. Every family handles conflict and communication different than the next, so it would behoove you to get to know and understand the way your boyfriend/ girlfriend or fiancé has been reared.

Here is a list of questions you may want to answer before entering into a serious relationship.[13]

1. Do you know his or her family values?

2. What kind of people raised this person I'm dating?
3. Does his or her family have negative habits?
4. Is there a history of verbal or physical abuse in his or her family?
5. How does his or her family handle conflict?
6. What are some of the hobbies his or her family has?
7. How would his or her family react to you marrying their son or daughter?
8. How does his or her family handle money?
9. Does his or her family practice the same faith as you?

Christy and I (Ryan) went on a cruise to the Bahamas and stayed in Miami Beach for our honeymoon, "Thanks Mom and Dad." It was beautiful. We went snorkeling and took pictures with an underwater camera. It was all we expected it to be. We were so anxious to show off our pictures and everything we bought on the trip. Unfortunately, this never happened because the bag (with all the pictures and Christy's clothes) was lost. The airline's final report said that it never even made it to the plane.

Sad and true story, but how awesome would it be if we could do that with all the heavy and negative baggage in our lives? What if we could just leave our distrust behind, leave our negative view and hurts life has dealt us, and just fly off without them? This is exactly what God would have us do. Why then does our baggage always seem to find it's way onto the plane with us? Honestly, it is because we are too afraid to part with it. It has become a crutch and many times we do not know how to operate with out it.

It took about a month before we settled with our home insurance company regarding our loss, so I (Christy) had to go that amount of time without my favorite jeans, or my best swimsuit. Sure it wasn't fun, especially when you want to look so great for your new spouse. But what a blessing to go out and get all new stuff once we settled. My friend Jesika and I had a blast on that shopping spree!

That is what God wants for you. Spend time with Him. Give your baggage over to Him and let Him inspect it. We guarantee He will not let you leave with anything that would harm you or anyone else on board. You must take care of your baggage before you enter into marriage. Check your bags in to God and don't look back. He disposed of them on the cross and He's waiting for you to hand them over.

We realize sometimes, that outside help is needed and often times the only way to heal. If this is the case, get it! Without a doubt everyone needs premarital counseling, but seriously consider personal counseling if you are carrying baggage of abuse or neglect that affects your current relationships. Remember everybody needs someone. Realize when you need outside help and get it. There is no shame in that, only honor.

Be sure and consider the source when seeking outside help. To really resolve these issues it takes skillful individuals who are trained in the area in which you need help. Co-workers, friends, and family members are not adequate counselors. They are too emotional and sometimes have their own agendas. Choose a qualified person outside of your personal life.

CHAPTER SEVEN

Let Me Tell Ya 'Bout The Birds and the Bees...

Sex

Let Me Tell Ya 'Bout The Birds and the Bees...

Sex

"Thou art fair, my love; there is no spot on thee."

-Song of Solomon 4:7 NKJ

I like him, I love him, I let him, I lose him.
-Anonymous

When God creates something, He creates it with purpose and design. The Genesis account of creation makes it clear that God's creation is *good* (Genesis 1:31). But mankind as a history of distorting what God has made, whether out of ignorance or just plain stubbornness. The golden calf of the Israelites is a prime example. Gold is beautiful to look at, but God clearly did not want His people worshipping it.

Sex (and yes, sex was God's idea) is no different. God created it, and therefore it is reasonable to expect that it is good. But when man distorts it by ignoring God's specific standards, it becomes harmful and destructive. So the question we've asked, "Why save sex for marriage?" is really a question of understanding God's purpose and design for sex. We can choose to do things *God's* way, and experience the beauty of His plan, or we can choose to do things *our* way, and experience harm and destruction (Proverbs 16:25).

So, let's talk first about why God created sex. One reason is obvious: procreation. When God told Adam and Eve to *"be fruitful and multiply"* (Genesis 1:28), they probably figured out that He wanted them to have sex. But God also wanted them to develop intimacy with one another, and He knew that sex would help them do that in a way that nothing else could. God also knew that because sex is so powerful in creating intimacy that there must be some constraints on how it was to be used, so He specifically relegated sex to the arena of marriage. The kind of intimacy that God desires between married couples cannot occur between one person and several others; it can only be experienced between *one* man and *one* woman. Hence one of the Ten Commandments, *"Do not commit adultery,"* (Exodus 20:14), and *"Flee sexual immorality,"* (1 Corinthians 6:18). That is, do not have sex with someone who is not your spouse. Obedience requires that sex be reserved for your spouse.

Couples must be very careful in being so flippant with such deep intimacy. Women especially, it is very different for you. Sex is the *closest bond* you can share physically with another person - no wonder we get so attached after engaging in sex. If you want to stay attractive, respected, and feel any sense of pride in yourself while in a relationship with someone, do not have sex with him or her.

So far we have two basic reasons to save sex for marriage: (1) God tells us to, and (2) God's purpose and design for sex cannot be fully achieved any other way. Many though, have argued that sex outside of marriage is not all that harmful. Let's look carefully at the potential consequences for this particular area of disobedience.

Sex without a good spiritual and emotional relationship is just like sneezing, it's just something that you get over with but it doesn't mean anything.

- Ann Landers

Sex outside of marriage causes damage in at least two areas: (1) physical consequences, things that affect your body and (2) relational consequences, things that affect your relationship.

YOUR BODY PAYS

The physical consequences are becoming increasingly obvious and increasingly dangerous in today's society. AIDS and other sexually transmitted diseases are frightening realities. "Safe sex" is more accurately described as "reduced risk sex." The only truly safe sex is abstinence. There is also a very real risk that children could be born - and possibly grow up without two parents. Your actions affect your life, your partner's life, and the lives of your family. They can result in handicapping an innocent baby's life as well. Worst of all the willful destruction of <u>human life</u> - abortion often results from pre-marital sex.

YOUR RELATIONSHIP PAYS

The relational consequences are just as real, though they may be more difficult to grasp. First, sin always damages a person's relationship with his God. Psalms 66:18 says, *"If I had cherished sin in my heart, the Lord would not have listened."*

Intentional disobedience of God's command to not commit *adultery* dishonors and displeases God. Conversely, God is pleased when His children choose obedience and self-control instead of the immediacy of pleasure.

Second, relational damage happens between a Christian and those who are watching his life. The sin of *adultery* (i.e. televangelist scandals) causes a person's friends and even "outsiders" to view the adulterer as *less* committed to obedience, and *more* prone to hypocrisy. But a Christian who saves himself or herself in obedience to God wins the respect of those who see his or her life.

Sex outside of marriage also damages the relationship between the persons involved. Trust is the main issue here. If two people do not cherish each other enough to wait for a marriage commitment before having sex, how can they trust one another for fidelity? After marriage, a man and woman build trust and respect for one another when they both survive the struggles of self-control - each will have the confidence that the other respects them, and cherishes their intimacy.

Similarly, if a person has not carried sexual purity into marriage, his or her marriage relationship is affected by the past. If a man or woman has previously had sex with someone else, their marital intimacy has already been affected. One or both spouses will have to deal with real or perceived comparisons with "former lovers" accompanied by a feeling that intimacy was not important enough for the other person to wait for it. But if both have waited for their wedding night, the intimacy has already begun with a solid foundation.

Why save sex for marriage? We've discussed several reasons…

(1) God commands us to.

(2) God's purpose and design for sex can only be achieved within marriage.

(3) Physical and relational consequences of sex outside of marriage are painfully real.

"But we're in love!" some might say. Maybe so, but if one believes in God's definition of love, he must realize that love is patient and kind; it does not seek to please itself, nor does it delight in evil, but is always hopeful (1 Corinthians 13). True love would be patient in waiting for the proper time for sex. It would be kind to future spouses by not pre-harming

marital intimacy. True love would be unselfish in placing God's desires and the needs of others above itself. It would not delight in the evil of disobedience, nor would it force another to disobey God. Love should never be a reason for premarital sex; rather, it should be one of the greatest reasons to *avoid* premarital sex.

"But we're going to be married anyway," is another common excuse. Along with being presumptuous, this stance will almost certainly leave one question unanswered: If one gives in to moral temptation before marriage, what's to stop him or her from giving in to moral temptation once married?

"What if it's too late? What if I've already forfeited my sexual purity?" Good question! Certainly a person cannot reverse the past, but there are a number of steps one should take to keep from further damaging his or her intimacy with God and others.

1. *Acknowledge your actions* as sin. For those who have accepted Christ's payment of the penalty for their sins, He asks only that they confess - agree with God that they are sinful (1John 1:9).

2. *Maintain purity* from this moment forward. Jesus told the woman caught in sexual sin to *"go and sin no more"* (John 8:11). You cannot change what's been done, but you can keep yourself and others from any further damage by avoiding situations, which might cause you to compromise your commitment to sexual purity. Paul advised Timothy to run away from temptation (2 Timothy 2:22), and Joseph is famous for running from moral danger (Genesis 39:7-12).

3. *Be honest* with anyone who is a "potential spouse" - don't wait till your wedding night to discuss your sexual past. Some intimacy problems may be averted if you address them early on.

4. *Forgive yourself* and ask God to give you a second virginity, a new place to begin again. He loves you and doesn't want you live in guilt - that is a trick of satan.

Receive your second virginity and maintain it.

Sex is a good thing. It must be, if God created it! The only way to keep it a "good thing" is to follow God's guidelines. He will reward you if you choose to honor Him and save sex for its proper time and place - your marriage.

CHAPTER EIGHT

Money, Money, Money, MONEY!

Finances and Relationships

Money, Money, Money, MONEY!

Finances and Relationships

"Beloved, I pray you may prosper in all things and be in health, just as your soul prospers."

-3 John 2 NKJ

The two things around which our Lord centered His most scathing teaching were money and marriage, because they are the two things that make men and women devils or saints.
-Oswald Chambers

The U.S. Congress stated in 2001 that the number one reason for arguments and relational problems is over money.[14] Think of couples you know, perhaps your parents, friends who are married, or couples in sitcoms or movies. How do they handle financial problems? Does our society deal with financial issues in a moral and intelligent manner? We want to make sure you are both on the same page concerning finances in your relationship.

We understand that if you are just dating, the issue of money may not come up that often. Be careful, you never know how quickly a *date* can turn into a *boyfriend/girlfriend*, then *fiancé*, and finally *husband or wife*. Do not be naïve in this area. The person you are in a relationship with may not have the same ideas about money, spending, or giving that you do. Have you ever talked about certain issues like who will do the bills? Will you have joint or separate checking accounts? Will you tithe? How much? Assuming that the other person has the same ideas that you have concerning finances is blinding yourself in a key area of your relationship.

You've probably heard people casually say, "Man, it would be so great to get paid just doin' what you love." Many times I (Christy) hear my father-in-law Richard quote the verse from Matthew chapter six, *"Where your treasure is, there your heart will be also."* However, he does not stop there. He goes on to reverse the statement to "where your *heart* is, there your *treasure* will be also". What he is saying is that a man must do what he loves. When God places a desire in your heart it is not to taunt you and make you miserable because you are not yet at that place in your life. He places the desire only to fulfill it, so you will be able to "do what you love."

In John Eldredge's book, Wild at Heart, he says that a man needs three things: a battle to fight, a beauty to rescue, and an adventure to live.[15] Men, if you are not living your adventure or fighting your battle at work, please stop and consider where you are going in life. You will be the leader of your family and they will look to you for direction through life. If you do not have a vision and goals for yourself, you will not have a vision or goals for your family. Most importantly, you will be miserable at your job and more than likely bring the misery home. Seek God's call on your life and *"neglect not the gift that is in you."* (I Timothy 4:14)

We are very blessed to be able to do what we love, minister. However, if Ryan needed to work at Taco Bell (my favorite place to eat) to put food on our table, he would do it in a heartbeat. The Bible is very clear on this subject. Take a look:

- II Thessalonians 3:10 *"...If any would not work, neither shall he eat."*

- I Timothy 5:8 *"But if any provide not for his own house, he hath denied the faith, and is worse than an infidel (non-believer)."*

I (Christy) really enjoy baking, mainly desserts and fun new recipes I find. Last Valentine's day I decided to bake heart-shaped cookies for Ryan (sugar cookies are his favorite). Long story short – the gesture may have been sweet, unfortunately the cookies were anything but. Mindlessly, I left out a key ingredient – sugar. Needless to say, the cookies went to waste. Like the sugar in sugar cookies, finances and money are key ingredients to discuss before entering a marriage. When left out, it just doesn't taste right.

Certain concepts, once mastered can give you much needed freedom in your relationship. We will discuss three concepts: tithing, money management, and generous giving.

TITHING

From as far back as I can remember, I (Christy) have tithed. Before I even began to earn my own money, I can remember my parents giving me 50 cents so I could stick it in an envelope at church and place it in the offering plate when it came down our isle. It was fun as a child, so I continued giving into my adult life. Ryan and I are both very grateful that our parents instilled the principle of tithing in us. However, when we were younger we tithed because it was the thing to do. It wasn't until later in our lives when we grew in Christ, that we learn the real reason for tithing.

This principle of tithing may not be a subject you have studied. It may even seem a bit foreign. So, let's take a look at what God has to say on the subject.

"'Bring all the tithes into the storehouse, that there may be food in My house, and try Me now in this', says the Lord of hosts, 'If I will not open for you the windows of heaven and pour out for you such a blessing that there will not be room enough to receive it'."

-Malachi 3:10 NKJ

Tithing is a spiritual law, which God commanded in the Old Testament (see Deuteronomy 26). In the verse preceding the one above God calls not tithing, *"robbing God."* You must grasp the concept that it is His money; not giving that to Him is not only *robbing Him*, but also *robbing you* of a blessed life.

In I Corinthians 1:20 it says that, "*...all the promises of God in Him are Yes, and in Him Amen, to the glory of God through us.*" God is true to His Word. He promises in Malachi chapter three that He will fill our storehouses, then rest assured, He will indeed fill our storehouses. Give in faith and speak the Word over your giving. Follow His command.

Ryan and I have been faithful in tithing and giving throughout our marriage and we have been blessed. God wants to bless you in your marriage as well. Make sure you and your partner are on the same page concerning tithing. Read Acts 5:1-11 about a couple who stole from God. Tithing may not seem like a moral issue, but God takes it very seriously. It is an act of honoring God with your possessions, and it is vital. Even when it seems hard, hold Him to His Word. Give and He will provide for you. For He is faithful!

MANAGING YOUR MONEY

What is the greatest law concerning money?

Whatever you have, spend less.

–In a letter from Samuel Johnson to a friend written March 20, 1782

Managing your money is almost as important as managing your marriage. And we do mean "your" money. The money should not be "his" or "hers," it belongs equally to you both. You are one in spirit and body. Your checking account should be the same. This can be difficult in situations where one person is a big spender while the other is very thrifty. Discuss these issues before you say the words "joint-checking" and you will eliminate problems before they start.

If you do not manage your money the problems can extend far beyond the account. Financial strains creep into relationships and can tear them apart. Make managing your money a priority. Don't expect it to just happen.

We have found that there is a certain cycle to money. It goes something like this: earned, managed, spent…earned, managed, spent…earned, managed, spent…and so on. Each person in the relationship is involved in at least one or maybe all steps in the cycle. Let's discuss the three steps in the cycle and who is involved with each one.

1. EARNED – Unless you are Joe Millionaire and have inherited millions, at some point you will have to earn a living in order to function in this world. Yes it takes money to live, and thank God, He always

provides. In today's times it is almost scary to step out on the limb and say what we are about to say. We believe that the man should be the provider for his home. Meaning that *he* is the major breadwinner. He works to support his wife and family. We are not saying that a woman should not be allowed to work by any means. We just believe that a woman should have the option to stay home if she chooses. Studies show children with a mother at home function better emotionally, physically, financially, and socially.

2. MANAGED – I (Ryan) asked Christy to marry me the fall semester of our senior year in college. The next semester (just before graduation) Christy and I both began working with Youth For Christ. This was before we were married in July. We purchased our home in June and with that came the expenses of furniture, insurance, vehicles, and everything that goes with it. We sat down one evening at my parent's home and designed a budget. Simply *living* can be a strain if you do not learn early on to cast your cares on God and trust Him with your future. God also wants us to use our gifts. Since sitting down to pay the bills each

month is a tough enough job, we decided to give that job to the most gifted person at money management. Ryan and I (Christy) had both managed our money in the past, but in all reality, Ryan was just the best man for the job (lucky him)! Choose the person in your relationship who will be the best at managing your money and paying the bills and allow them to utilize their gifts.

3. SPENT – After going on just a few dates with Ryan, I (Christy) found out that he was a much bigger spender than I was. Ryan would always get the "combo meal" when I ordered a "Whopper Junior" with water. If your relationship is halfway normal, one of you will probably be a bigger spender than the other. That's okay, but be wise. Spend wisely. Talk about expenses and things you would desire to have. Overspending can cause many problems in a relationship as can one person who is too tight with money. Make sure you and the person you are dating agree on the type of lifestyle you want to have, and iron out the issues of spending. If you don't, you can run into problems that cost you more than money can

buy - your marriage or your family. Talk about money and how you will spend it with your partner now. Don't wait until creditors are hounding you and bills are piling up.

The god of materialism offers nothing permanent to the woman who succumbs to it. She does not view the past with satisfaction because she never got all she wanted. The present is unappreciated, because her whole focus is on the future.

- Barbara Bush

GIVING

Giving is different than tithing. Giving is over and above your tithe. It is being able to bless others.

"Give and it will be given unto you: good measure, pressed down, shaken together, and running over shall men give unto your bosom. For with the same measure that you use, it will be measured back to you"

-Luke 6:38 NKJ

Because of our faithfulness God made it possible for us to buy my (Christy) younger brother Tim a car after he got his license. I think that doing that blessed us more than it even blessed Tim. God blesses us so we can bless *others*. After all, He doesn't say that we are his hands and his feet for no reason, we are. Be a giver. Give generously and often. Don't be stingy and selfish. Follow the lead of the Leader and be a giver.

If you only have enough to meet your own needs, how can you bless anyone else?
-Christy Tate

Below is a quick test to see how'"right on" you and your mate are with money. Take this test and see where you stand. Make adjustments now and don't wait until problems creep into your life. Satan wants you to fail in these areas so you will not have a blessed life. Don't let him get the best of your financial situation…fight back!

(Answer the following statements with yes or no)

TITHING

1. I tithe at least 10% of my gross pay.

   You_____ Boyfriend/Girlfriend _____

2. I tithe consistently (monthly / weekly).

   You_____ Boyfriend/Girlfriend_____

MONEY MANAGEMENT

1. I currently operate on a budget.

   You_____ Boyfriend/Girlfriend_____

2. I have and use multiple credit cards.

   You_____ Boyfriend/Girlfriend_____

3. I value nice things & care about appearance.

   You_____ Boyfriend/Girlfriend_____

GIVING

1. I believe God will bless me according to my willingness to give to Him.

   You_____ Boyfriend/Girlfriend_____

2. I take pride in giving to others in need.

   You_____ Boyfriend/Girlfriend_____

3. I am a giving person (not stingy/selfish).

   You_____ Boyfriend/Girlfriend_____

How did you do? How did your boyfriend/girlfriend do? Did you match up? Do you have some questions and things to discuss with them? If so, do not put them off. Talk about it!

Remember this! All you have is not really yours – it ALL belongs to God. So be grateful. Christy shared with me (Ryan) a saying that her Grandpa Don always said, "The greatest sin of our nation is not murder or idolatry. It is ingratitude." We must be grateful for all that we have. We live in a blessed, blessed nation where we have the freedom to openly ask God to make all of the desires of our hearts become a reality. If you keep a grateful heart you will tithe and be a giver. But most importantly, you will be free from selfishness and stinginess. Be grateful.

"Every good and perfect gift is from above, and comes down from the Father of lights, with whom there is no variation or shadow of turning."

-James 1:2 NKJ

CHAPTER NINE

I Say A Little Prayer For You...

Dealing With Spiritual Issues

I Say A Little Prayer For You...

Dealing with Spiritual Issues

"Endeavoring to keep the unity of the Spirit in the bond of peace".

-Ephesians 4:3 NKJ

God and love are synonymous. Love is not an attribute of God, it is God.
-Oswald Chambers

If this book could only be one chapter long, this would be the chapter we would choose for you to read. Why? Because every issue you face in life is a spiritual issue. Every problem in life boils down to a spiritual problem. For instance in marriage, if Christy and I (Ryan) are in an argument it is usually the result of a character flaw (spiritual issue) in one or both of us.

At the root of every problem is a character flaw.

-Ryan and Christy Tate

In choosing a husband or wife, picture yourself broken, bleeding, hurt, and in the deepest ditch of your life (this part isn't fun). Maybe you are diagnosed with a disease, you lose your job after 30 years, or worse yet you lose a family member. Is the person you are with right now the person you want by your side? Will they mourn with you or distance themselves? Will they lift you up or fall deeper into depression with you? Will they be there? Would you be comfortable being completely transparent with them? These are the situations in life that you must prepare for. We are not prophesying doom over your life, but we want you to take a deeper look into the person with whom you're choosing to spend your life. Will they have your back through the battles that life presents?

My (Christy) father fought in the Vietnam conflict (1970-71). During the war he received many medals, including a purple heart. My dad also received a bronze star with a "V" for Valor. This was awarded for saving a man's life during battle. The medal my dad won indeed was a great honor, but nothing compared to the joy the family had when their son came home. Who you have fighting beside you can either save your life or get you killed.

Choosing who fights beside you is just as important, or even more important than how you fight the battle. In a war, you have little choice as to who stands next to you, but in life's battles we are free to choose our fellow battlers. We choose how we fight the battle and whom we fight alongside. We will discuss these two critical areas.

The Battle

Have you ever noticed that in the Old Testament of the Bible it seems that the Israelites were always in a battle of some sort? There were many wars among them and their tribes. Read the book of Joshua for some examples. Do you ever feel that your life goes the same way? Do you feel like you awake every day in a war zone?

Life is a series of battles. Likewise your love life and marriage will be presented with many challenging battles. Some you may win easily – others will be difficult, but the battle is worth it! Rest in the fact that God has promised to fight for us!

"...For the battle is not yours, but God's"

-II Chronicles 20:15 NKJ

Every couple's battle is different. You may be trying to get through school, looking for a job, raising a family, or searching for purpose in your life. Regardless of how big or small, everyone has battles they must fight in life. But more important than fighting the battle is *winning* the battle. If you are fighting to get your life into a position where you have peace and happiness, but keep butting your head up against a wall, it is probably because you have not grasped a very important concept found in a letter written by a man named Paul about 2000 years ago. This is what he writes:

"For we are not wrestling with flesh and blood (contending only with physical opponents), but against the despotisms, against the powers, against (the master spirits who are) the world rulers of this present darkness, against the spirit forces of wickedness in the heavenly (supernatural) spheres." -Ephesians 6:12 AMP

Make no mistake, every encounter you have during the day or even in your relationship that tests your patience, your integrity, or even your thoughts is a chance for you to fight and win a supernatural battle. Everyday you go to battle. Satan wakes up every morning and plots an attack on your life. And until you awaken to the fact that he wants you destroyed (John 10:10) then you will continue to lose battles and fall short of victory in your life.

God has a plan for your life. He wants to reveal it to you, but satan is in the business of blinding us and tempting us with his own shortcuts along the way. To beat him we must *wage war* against satan and be on the offense. You must have a spiritual partner fighting with you.

Your Partner

I (Christy) loved my elementary school, Bryant Elementary. I can't think of much I would have changed about that school except one little part. During P.E. we would always play kickball (just like baseball expect there are no bats and you kick instead). The gym teacher would always chose two team captains and then they would take turns picking their team one by one until there wasn't anyone left to choose. I don't know why, but every time we played I was always chosen last. In all actuality I know why, the team captain wanted to win the game. I was small and couldn't kick the ball very hard. The captain chose the best players to have a better chance of winning. The same is true in life. Choose your team carefully.

II Corinthians 6:14 states, *"Do not be unequally yoked together with an unbeliever."* If you enter the battle of life with an unbeliever, you will be on your own in *every* battle. Choose a helpmate, not a hurt-mate.

The choice is yours. Who will you *choose* to help win the battle of parenting and rearing your child? Who will you *choose* to help win the battle over a child that is in rebellion? Who will you *choose* to help win a battle over an empty bank account? Who will you *choose* to help you win the battle of living your dreams? Choose wisely and choose to win! Let's take a look at what a good soldier looks like.

A Good Soldier...

KNOWS HIS ENEMY

First and foremost, a good soldier is trained to be the best he can be. He also knows his mission and purpose: to defeat the enemy. If you are in a relationship with someone who has not recognized the enemy (an unbeliever), be careful, they will not know when or where to fire and when they do it might be at you. Worse than that, they will just sit behind while you walk into the field and go it alone.

WEARS HIS ARMOR

Second, a good soldier never goes into war without the proper armor. There is different armor for different battles. For instance, a soldier fighting in the desert during the Gulf War would not wear the same fatigues of one fighting in the jungles of Vietnam. Different battles require different armor. Nowhere is the armor for spiritual battle outlined better than in Ephesians 6. Read verses 13-18. Put on this armor and choose a partner who understands the importance of wearing it as well. Here is a break down of the armor we should put on daily:

- Belt of Truth
- Breastplate of Righteousness
- Shod your feet with the Gospel
- Shield of Faith
- Helmet of Salvation

- Sword of the Spirit (Word of God)
- Prayer

MASTERS HIS WEAPONS

Third, a good soldier knows how to use his weapons. God has equipped every Christian with the same weapons. We will discuss four major weapons the Lord has given us.

Prayer -

We have a direct line of communication with God. Prayer is one of our greatest assets and one of our strongest weapons. I (Ryan) cannot express what a blessing it is to be able to reach over, grab Christy's hand, and not even have to mention what I need: a prayer partner. In James 5:15 the word tells us' *"the prayer of faith will save the sick."* Prayer is an awesome weapon God gives us as believers, and it is adequate for many battles. The Bible says that in prayer we can call on angels. Deuteronomy 32:30 tells us that one can set a thousand to flight, but two can set 10,000 to flight. Marry someone who will battle with you in prayer.

Fasting -

A second weapon is one Jesus discusses in Matthew 17:21. Jesus tells his disciples that this battle cannot be won *"...except by prayer and fasting."* Fasting is another weapon we can use. This is little used discipline, but can be a powerful tool of weaponry. Jesus fasted for 40 days and 40 nights before He was tempted by the devil in the wilderness. Fasting is a weapon adequate for many battles in life. It shows sacrifice and honor to God. Those who fast are truly blessed.

The Word of God -

This weapon is referred to in the sixth chapter of Ephesians as a sword. John 6:63 says, *"...the Words I speak to you are spirit, they are life."* God's Word is living and alive. It is knowledge and power. In the beginning, God *spoke* and there was light. He spoke things into existence, and He spoke His Word to men who wrote through divine inspiration. As you read His Word and study it, a change will begin in you. As you apply His Word to your life it will begin to change your situations. And as you speak it to your enemy and claim the promises in His Word, you will begin to win your battles.

Hosea 4:6 says, *"My people are being destroyed for a lack of knowledge."* Do not let this become the legacy of your family.

The Holy Spirit -

In the Old Testament, God dwelt in the Ark of the Covenant here on earth. During the New Testament He lived on earth as a man named Jesus. In the present, He lives inside of those who believe in Him. When you become born again God places His Holy Spirit to live inside of you. The Holy Spirit is not only a weapon, but primarily our Chief Commander. If we were the Marines, He would be our Commandant.

If you are dating someone who is not a Christian, or are considering dating someone who is not a Christian, remember that they do not have the Holy Spirit living in them. Before you decide to be with someone who does not have God's Spirit living in him or her, read on.

The ministry of the Holy Spirit is threefold. He lives in men to convict them, to reveal things to them, and to divinely empower them. All three of these aspects of the Holy Spirit are vital in a marriage and in a working and functioning relationship.

1. *Conviction* – As a woman, I (Christy) do not like the word "nag" being associated with being a woman. Why are we labeled this way? Women, I'm sorry but I believe it is because that is what's in our nature to do. It comes from a desire to fix, nurture, and keep our families and relationships at peace. Do not get in the habit of doing this. Marry someone who already has the Holy Spirit living in them so you won't feel the need to be their Holy Spirit. What an awesome revelation when you can let go of your boyfriend/ girlfriend or fiancé and let the Holy Spirit work on them. If you are not in a relationship with a believer, they do not have the Holy Spirit. You must make the choice to become a nag, live in distress, or end the relationship.
2. *Revelation & Guidance*– By revelation we do not mean that we look into a crystal ball and see what our future will look like. It is much deeper and more beautiful than that. In I Corinthians chapter two, the Bible says that God has revealed His plans to us through His Spirit. In Proverbs 25:2 it says, *"It is the glory of God to conceal a matter, but it is the glory of*

kings to search a matter out." What a comfort to know that your husband or wife is being led down the right path. Ladies are you content with following the leading of the man you are with right now? How are they leading their own life? What is their vision, their dreams, their calling? Do you see yourself following the same ones? Guys, does the woman you are with right now take pleasure in godly things or worldly things? Does she follow crowds that bring her true joy or temporary pleasure? Would she support your vision and calling? Your future lies in the hands of your husband or wife to be, as well as the lives of your future children. I (Christy) have so much joy and I am so grateful that I can rest in the fact that Ryan listens to the Holy Spirit. I let the Holy Spirit be the nag so I don't have to!

3. *Divine Empowerment—"But you shall receive power when the Holy Spirit has come upon you..."*(Acts 1:8). There are many ways in which the Holy Spirit can empower men and women. We will touch on only *one* of the many. We want to discuss how the Holy Spirit can empower a person to *love*. To understand

> true love you must understand God, because God is love. When God sent His Son Jesus to die on the cross in our place, He demonstrated perfect love. *"Greater love hath no man than this, that a man lay down his life for his friends."* (John 15:13) That is exactly the love that God showed to mankind. If a person has not experienced this love from God, there is no way they can give it. Unconditional love between two people is only found when both are believers and can exercise mercy, grace, and forgiveness. The Word of God says that *"love covers a multitude of sins,"* (I Peter 4:8) and that *"perfect love casts out all fear"*(I John 4:18). To experience a marriage of true love is to experience marriage with a believer.

Everything is spiritual. Every life situation and trial you go through is spiritual. So to go through life with someone who is not in the battle with you can be devastating. Who is beside you?

This chapter may be a lot to swallow, but it is essential to a successful relationship. It is easy to read about dating only Christians and people who challenge you spiritually, and it is easy to talk about the person you will marry as a spiritual giant. The hard part is applying the principles you already know. No one can make you do this. You must decide on your own that you will not settle for anything less than what God wants for you. If you believe in God then you should have the faith that He has someone out there for you. The person He has chosen for you He has also chosen for Himself. Let God fix him or her and all that's left for you to do is to make sure that your eyes are open to recognizing your true mate when they are revealed to you.

Can we be real with you for a moment? *Dating non-Christians leads to marrying non-Christians.* Below is what we like to call a checklist for spiritual dating. You may just be dating and not considering marriage with this person, you may be engaged or maybe you are single right now. This checklist will work for all of you.

CHECKLIST

1. Have "that" talk – discuss personal beliefs
2. Worship Together – choose a church
3. Pray Together
4. Be on the Same Team – share a vision

To have a successful relationship you must connect on many levels. The most vital level on which to connect is the spiritual - this is where every other issue begins. Remember, God is on your side on this. He wants you to find the right person with whom to tie the knot. Ask for help from Him and let Him guide you. He will. Pray as Jesus did in Matthew 6:10, *"Your will be done on earth as it is in heaven."*

We can be confident that His desire to reveal will always be greater than our desire to know.

-Carrie Anna Pearce

CHAPTER TEN

Love Shack Baby...

Truths About Living Together

Love Shack Baby...

Truths About Living Together

"Great peace have they which love Thy law..."

-Psalm 119:165 NKJ

The woman who wants to make a difference must seek inner strength instead of self-sufficiency.

-Joyce B. Gage

We might as well call this what most call it today - "shackin' up." Sort of crude isn't it? The term originated out of the '60's culture that found so many people of both sexes living in the same place - often the place was not much more than a shack because hardly anyone had the money to pay for rent. "Shackin' up" came to mean just a man and woman living together outside of marriage. Although the practice is wide-spread and even socially acceptable today it is not acceptable to God, and we will examine some myths that young people believe about the benefits of "living together" outside of a sacred marriage. Webster defines, cohabitation as "living together as or as if husband and wife." It follows then, that those who are living together *as husband and wife*, are having sexual relationship *as husband and wife* do. Many times one party demands the other to "live together" as proof of love.

Those who live together without marriage do not experience God's best for their lives individually or together. Usually men and women have different reasons for justifying "living together." Studies have found that men typcially agree to live together because of the convenience of the relationship, whereas, women do it with the expectation that it will lead to marriage.[16]

The month before we married, we finished building our first new house. It was brand new and filled with furniture, paintings, and wedding gifts that we had already received from friends and family. I (Ryan) asked Christy if I could stay there until the wedding and she was adamant. "No," she said. She didn't even want us to be in the house together until our wedding later in the month. I wasn't even allowed to sit and bounce up and down on the new bed to try it out. Why? It was non-negotiable with her because she wanted us to have the special experience together when we first entered the house *as husband and wife*. I will never forget how precious that day was when I carried my bride across the threshold of our home.

Let's look at some of the things couples lie to themselves about to justify living together. These are based on current popular myths.

The truth is that wherever a man lies with a woman, there, whether they like it or not, a transcendental relation is set up between them which must be eternally enjoyed or eternally endured.

-C.S. Lewis, Screwtape Letters

MYTHS ABOUT LIVING TOGETHER BEFORE MARRIAGE

Myth # One:
"Everybody's Doing It!"

You'd sometimes think so, but actually everybody is not "doing it." Statistics[17] show that of college-age people, 65 to 80 percent are sexually active and some of those are living together. Estimates are that 30 to 40 percent of college students live together during their time at college. Although this is a large number, this also indicates that around 20 to 35 percent are not sexually active and somewhere around 60 to 70 percent of students do not decide to live together. "Everybody's doing it," is a myth and does not hold up.

Myth # Two:
"We're Not Hurting Anyone"

Really? Ask some of the couples who spent years together, with one thinking that the relationship would lead to marriage. It ends, one partner walks away free, while the other is devastated. Not hurt? Get real! People are hurt, either emotionally, physically, or both. Even those not directly involved such as friends and family may be hurt as well. Sin is like throwing a pebble in the pond, it sends ripples across the entire pond. Sin is never solitary, it always has a "rippling effect." The consequences of our choices can be extremely painful. Living together can make one party feel totally used sexually or emotionally and that hurts. It also hurts parents who have prayed that their children would remain pure sexually until marriage. Society says it is no big deal and that we can have pleasure without commitment. But sex is a powerful emotional bond. God has put constraints on it and asks only that we relegate it into an exclusive union - marriage. Living together and the sexual bond it creates may devalue the person later, cause emotional hurt, and may seriously effect the health and well being of one or both parties involved.

Myth # Three:
"Financially It Is Advantageous"

We have all heard the old adage that it is cheaper for two to live together, than one. That may be true in some instances, however, monetary savings cannot be compared to the "sell out" of ones own moral standards - virginity and purity. Also, couples who live together do not "share" financial resources. Often, he has *his* money, she has *hers*. There is no common responsibility to each other in this area, whereas in a marriage relationship, ideally it is *our* money. Many times one party in the living together situation feels that they are taken advantage of financially by the other. Then when they split, one is left in financial ruin. Kevin Leman in his book, "*Smart Kids, Stupid Choices*" states, "It's kind of like giving someone a million dollars and later finding out you gave it to the wrong person, but now he's gone and so is your money. Gone for good. You don't have it anymore. And the person who should have had it will now never get it."

Myth # Four:
"It's Nobody's Business"

Nothing could be further from the truth. First of all, it is *society's business.* America was founded on Christian principles that exonerated marriage and family. Living together says, “we do not honor the basic tenents that made this country strong. The old standard is too rigid, sexual purity is not important.” Societal ills, including babies born to unwed mothers, and fathers not responsible for children, are direct results of “living together” situations. It is also the *church’s business*. The church should be doing a better job teaching young people about sexual issues and pre-marriage decisions that cause negative consequences. Lastly, it is *God’s business*. God is seriously interested in what we do with every part of our lives. He greatly desires that we avoid the pitfalls of sex before marriage and the hurt and regret it can cause. He loves us so much and yearns for us to know the benefits and joy of simple obedience to His word. Marriage alone should provide the environment of trust, security, and stability for both parties - one in which children will be nurtured and feel safe as well.

Myth # 5:
“It’s All-Right Because We’re In Love and We’re Going To Get Married Anyway”

Living together has come to mean a “try out” or “testing” time. There is usually one party who does not think of a permanent marriage relationship - some are just standing by until someone better comes along. But, let's just say that you really believe it's love. Is love alone a reason for premarital sex or living together? Love is actually the greatest reason to refrain from sex outside of marriage. The scripture in Romans 13 says love is patient and kind. So, if it is love, you will be patient and wait for the proper time for sex, etc. Let us throw in something here that hopefully you will understand - love can be tricky! That's right. Feelings can fool you. Discussed elsewhere in this book are the differences between love and infatuation - divided sometimes by only a very thin line. Add to that sexual intimacy and the issues get really clouded. Sex makes you feel closer than you actually are...and can make you feel as if you are in love, when actually you are just in sex!

God's word is clear - sex outside of marriage is "fornication" a word that actually came from the Greek word 'porneia' meaning prostitution. God chose that strong word to describe sexual activity without marriage. If you are just satisfying lust and passion - that isn't love.[18] Anyone can do that - God has something better for you. True love doesn't settle and just move in together - true love waits!

Myth # Six:

"The Bible Doesn't Say We Have To Have a Ceremony to Be Married"

The Bible indeed does address the institution of marriage in Genesis 2. In biblical times there was a contractual agreement, sometimes verbal that signified a marriage. Jesus was attending a wedding ceremony when he turned the water into wine. Marriages took place at a certain time and place. Marriage ceremonies were expected.

"Fornication" is the biblical term for sexual activity outside of marriage. And the Bible says, "no." Look at I Corinthians 7:2, *"...but, because of fornications, let each man have his own wife, and let each woman have her own husband."* Paul is writing here saying that marriage is in contrast to fornication, and fornication can be avoided by getting married. Paul even suggests strongly that those believers who don't have self control to live the single life, need to marry. (I Corinthians 7:9). Further proof God is very interested in your marriage is the fact that he refers to us, his chosen people, as His "*bride*" and He, our *"bridegroom."* All born-again Christians are even invited to the *"marriage supper of the Lamb."*

"Blessed are they which are called unto the marriage supper of the Lamb."

–Revelation 19:9 NKJ

Myth #7:

"The Marriage License Is Only A Piece of Paper Anyway...and we don't need a piece of paper to prove our love."

This is spoken by people who try to convince themselves and others that if they live together they are married in the sight of God- the license isn't necessary. If you want to follow that "proving your love" thing – then never buy a ring - a ring is a symbol that could be mistaken for proof of love. No, what this person is actually saying is, "I don't want to make promises I may not be able to keep; I love you, but I don't know about committing in front of God and witnesses for a life-time; I love you, but not enough to give you my last name; I love you, but the marriage ceremony gives honor, respect and dignity to a relationship - I don't know if I love you that much." Most importantly, don't forget that a marriage license is still the law in most states for legitimizing a union. Our government has made a marriage license a civil requirement. Why not just obey the law?

Myth # Eight:
"Living Together Will Give Me Security and Raise My Self-Esteem"

If sex were just that and nothing more, it would be so much easier. But real people are involved in real situations where they become emotionally, physically, and mentally attached to another human being. You are a part of every person you have had sexual relations with and they are a part of you. Think about it, especially you guys or gals who "sleep around" a lot. Here you have given yourself to many, many people trying to find love, trying to find security, and what do you have to show for it? A bad reputation, low self-worth, feelings of loss, abandonment, or the sense of being used. You have given yourself away, one "piece" at a time. The result is that you are no longer "whole." How can you be?

Parts of you are missing. Living together doesn't bolster self esteem or security - quite the opposite - you feel less self-worth and the security you are seeking will always be elusive because you or the other person is unwilling to commit wholeheartedly to a marriage relationship.

Some Interesting Statistics About Living Together [19]

- Before 1960 co-habitation was uncommon, but by the mid 1990's more than 50% of couples were choosing to live together before or in place of marriage
- Sexually active unmarried women are almost four times more likely to be under psychiatric care
- Women who are in a living together situation have rates of depression 3 times higher than married women
- Woman are 62% more likely to be assaulted by a live-in boyfriend than by a husband
- 40% of women living with boyfriend were forced to endure sex they disliked or was abusive

- The Canadian government agency Statscan report stated that in a one year period, one in every five women who live in common law realtionships are assaulted, and those with male partners under age 25 are most at risk [20]
- Child abuse is nearly twenty times higher in cases when a couple is "living together"
- 72% of 1,200 teens, ages 12 to 17 years old said they agree with pro-abstinence message, but 44% said we hear too little about how or why to say no to sex [21]

*ICR Survey Research Group, U.S. Justice Department, Family Violence Research Program, Pediatrics Magazine

Ask anyone who is married today and you will get the same anwer, "I wouldn't trade my time living alone for anything." It is not that they do not love their husband or wife and their family, but there is just something about the *time* you have alone that teaches you to appreciate your relationships more. Growing up, I can remember my (Christy) youth minister's wife responding to us in the youth group when someone would complain about being too busy to study.

She would say, "You think you're busy now? Wait until you are married and have children." She was right.

The single life is a gift. Enjoy it! When you marry it will be until death do you part, that means living together for the rest of your lives. Why would you want to throw away the years of growth and personal time God has blessed you with? Maybe you're fearful that your relationship will not work out and that is why you are rushing to save it by pouring out all that you have and all that you are. Please, do not invite that kind of heartache.

Be smart and mature. Be grateful of this time that you have, you only have it once and then it is gone. And when it is time to give your self to someone, make sure they are worth it!

CHAPTER ELEVEN

The Test...

Is It True Love?

The Test...

Is It True Love?

"There is no fear in love; but perfect love casts out fear"

–I John 4:18 NKJ

Love is difficult to define, but the working definition I would like to give is that "Love is the sovereign preference of one person for another person".
– Oswald Chambers

What if there was a test for true love? In fairy tales true love was proven by a kiss on the lips of "Sleeping Beauty" or "Snow White." In "Beauty and the Beast," the words "I love you," transformed the hideous beast into a handsome Prince. Are we able to determine true love by a kiss or words alone? Can we know for sure if someone really loves us? Can we tell when someone is just using love words but doesn't have a clue what real love means? Are they just saying the words they believe we want to hear?

Romantic minds want the kiss, the touch, the look, the encounter to be "magical" and wham! It hits us between the eyes - true love. Getting real, however means that we realize those things are wonderful and can add to a love relationship, but *real* love is proven by other methods.

In fact, there is a test – a true love test. Tucked into the pages of Apostle Paul's letter to the Corinthian church is a beautiful, no-nonsense test to determine true love. There are eleven parts on the test. Flunk any part and you flunk it all – Why? Because every part is essential to the whole. You don't pick and choose which ones you want to be pretty good at and those you will skip over, or make up later. Every element of the test matters. Think you're in love? Let's see.

1. TRUE LOVE IS PATIENT.

(I Corinthians 13:4)

Most of us bristle at the word, patient. This "get it now or lose out" society is not prone to patience. Webster defines patience as follows.

"...To demonstrate calmness, self-control, and the willingness or ability to tolerate delay."

Have you ever tried to shake an hourglass to get the sand to fall through faster? Doesn't work. The hourglass was designed to allow the sand through grain by grain until it empties into the other end. God's plan for you is the hour glass and, like the sand, we are passing through events and time as He wills - try to rush it or skip the process and you are on your own. Patience is allowing God's perfect will to be the priority of your life no matter how long the process takes. With that in mind, when testing true love, patience is essential in three critical ways:

First, be patient until the "right" person comes along. Don't get frustrated and settle for less than you want in a guy or girl because you want someone NOW. *"Maybe, the person I have been looking for, praying for only exists in my mind,"* you say, or *"Why doesn't God bring that person into my life'– am I not being a good enough Christian or something?"*

It is imperative as you seek true love to realize that God promises us *"the desires of our hearts."* (Psalm 37:4). But the required action that goes with that verse is the first part, look at the direction —*"Delight yourself in the Lord,*

THEN He will give you the desires of your heart." Patience is demonstrated by "delighting yourself in the Lord" *while* you are waiting on true love. How do you do that?

To "delight in the Lord" means to make Him the focus of your life – not whether or not you have a boyfriend or girlfriend. Do you know those people who HAVE to be dating someone or "going out" with someone to feel desirable or secure? In dating situations, those who seem desperate, are often times less attractive. You see them everywhere. These are the guys or girls who can't be alone so they come on too strong and pushy. They are desperate for affection, desperate for attention, and these are the people who *have* a problem so they will *be* a problem!

Being patient and "delighting in the Lord" also means to be all about growing in your understanding of Him. It means getting into His Word and learning about Him, discovering what it means to be a prayer warrior, and concentrating on watching God work in your life. Further down in verse 7 of Psalm 37, the Word instructs us to *"Be still before the Lord and wait patiently for Him."* That's it! You can't really "delight yourself" in God when you are angry and impatient all the time.

Sure, it's difficult to want a Christian girl or guy and seemingly there are none in sight. But it will be worth the wait. Don't settle for just anyone, be patient for the one who is right for you. Just because they are not there staring you in the face doesn't mean they don't exist. He/She is out there somewhere and in God's time they will show up. Just make sure that you are working on being the kind of person God wants you to be when they do come along. In the meantime go on with your life and live your vision and purpose while you are waiting. Never put your life on hold just because you are waiting on a relationship to happen. Be about "delighting yourself in the Lord" and you will be the happy, successful single that is most attractive and desirable to other singles.

Another kind of patience - Are you patient in the area of sexual gratification? Do you refuse to give in to society's pull to be sexually active before marriage? Waiting is a sign of true love. It is putting value on a special part of a relationship that God intended for a married couple to experience. Elsewhere in this book, this subject is examined but for our purposes in this section, it takes concerted and intense effort and commitment spiritually, emotionally, and physically to be patient and forego sexual gratification until marriage – that is God's perfect plan.

Finally, are you developing the overall virtue of patience in all relationships? The guy or girl who is impatient with his little sister, or volatile with his parents is not exhibiting patience. Does he/she have an anger problem? Watch closely how she treats those within her family and her friends. Are they patient with the weak, the young, and the elderly? Just because he/she is patient with you at present does not mean that down the road they won't reveal their true self.

True love exists when a person's words and deeds reflect they are controlled, loving, and considerate of others.

** Grading Scale:*

A - Excellent, B - Good, C - Average,

D- Needs improvement, F - Fail

PATIENCE

Your Grade ______ **His/Her Grade_____**

2. TRUE LOVE IS KIND.

(I Corinthians 13:4)

Kindness, simply put, is being interested in the needs, the hurts, and the lives of others before your own. It is saying or doing the thing that will make someone else happy. Mother Theresa said, "Let no one ever come to you without leaving better and happier. Be the living expression of God's kindness: in your face, in your eyes, in your smile."

True love exhibits acts of kindness continually. I (Ryan) came back from a very tiring day to find this note on my desk . We had produced a major golf tournament/fundraiser and I was drained physically and emotionally. This "act of kindness" in the form of a note from my wife made it all seem worthwhile. True love does things like this all the time:

Ryan, today was full of fun and happiness for so many people because of you. The tournament was perfect. You did an excellent job and I am soooo proud of you!!!! I love you, Ryan Tate. Good Work!

Love, your wife,
Christy

Here are a few questions to ask to determine if you or the person you are interested in, is exhibiting genuine kindness:

1. Is he/she cruel to innocent or weak people?
2. Am I sometimes cruel?
3. Is he/she controlling – always checking up on you, where you go, who you are with - suspicious. Is this person you?
4. Is she/he jealous of your relationships with other people, even your family? Protects you from others, "for your own good?"
5. Am I the jealous one? Do I try to isolate her/him?

Kindness is a godly trait that you can develop. It is the desire to meet the needs of those around you. William Penn, one of our forefathers, said it best…

> "I expect to pass through this world but once. Any good therefore that I can do, or any kindness that I can show to any fellow creature, let me do it now. Let me not defer or neglect it, for I shall not pass this way again."

KINDNESS

Your Grade______ His/Her Grade_____

3. TRUE LOVE DOES NOT ENVY.

(I Corinthians 13:4)

To envy another in a relationship is to be intimidated, or may even feel threatened by them. If you are envious, you cannot celebrate their accomplishments or gifts. The envious person is constantly putting the other down to build himself/herself up. The envious person is selfish, disrespectful, prideful, and constantly competing for attention.

True love is not envious. That means you rejoice when the other wins and you are genuinely happy for them. You find ways to admire and respect who they are - you speak words of affirmation to them. You are their greatest cheerleader. If this trait is not exhibited in a dating relationship you can be sure it will not show up in marriage. Marry the person who is envious and you are setting yourself up to be constantly berated, and knocked down emotionally.

Also, the envious person is never satisfied with what she/he has. They always want what someone else has. They live their lives dissatisfied with who they are, failing to embrace the person God created them uniquely to be. True love considers the gifts and accomplishments of the other to be his/her own and celebrates accordingly.

DOES NOT ENVY

Your Grade_____ His/Her Grade_____

4. TRUE LOVE IS NOT JEALOUS.

(I Corinthians 13:4)

Jealousy is referred by many as "the green eyed monster." And what a monster it can be in your relationship when one or both parties are""possessed" by this evil ogre. Sometimes we excuse jealousy by saying, "Well, you don't really love someone if you aren't a little jealous now and then." Totally not true. True love believes the other, trusts them, and is absolutely sure of their affection, their motives, and their loyalty.

The following is a list of some signs that may indicate that you or your dating interest is bent toward jealousy:

1. Are they constantly interrogating you if you are late or not at home?
2. Is he/she controlling?
3. Do they check up to see where you go? Who you are with?

4. Do they insist you check with them before you go anywhere?
5. Do they attempt to isolate you from other friends – or family? May even say they are "protecting you" from people who are not good for you?
6. Do they show up unexpectedly trying to catch you doing something wrong?
7. Do they check your phone call list, or even your car mileage?
8. Do they get angry if you spend time with anyone other than him/her?
9. Are they repentant when they act jealous - but say it is your fault?

JEALOUSY

Your Grade____ **His/Her Grade_____**

5. TRUE LOVE IS NOT PRIDEFUL.

(I Corinthians 13:4)

We should remind ourselves often of the scripture that talks about pride. Proverbs 11:2 says,

"Pride goes before destruction, and a haughty spirit before a fall." Are you setting yourself up for a huge fall because you have so much pride? Usually the person who is prideful can never admit they are wrong.

The prideful person is consumed with looking right, feeling right, and being right at all costs. They demonstrate little mercy. They rarely ask for forgiveness for anything, because they truly believe they cannot be wrong!

Humility is one of the attributes of Christ but the prideful person sees humility as weakness or frailty. Marry a prideful person and his/her harsh and unyielding spirit will make the entire family miserable.

PRIDEFUL

Your Grade_____ His/Her Grade_____

6. TRUE LOVE IS NOT RUDE.

(I Corinthians 13:5)

I don't think we have to define rudeness to anyone – you know it when you see it, or feel it. It hurts. The rude person says things that demean, disregard, depress, or hurt. They do things to inflict pain and seemingly never regret them. They are insulting in private and in public. Here are a few of the things that should be red flags to signal that you or your dating interest is basically a rude individual.

The rude person:[22]

- Ridicules and berates in public
- Rolls his/her eyes, smirks at others remarks
- Interrupts often - does not listen
- Makes fun of others clothes, hair, etc.
- May be racist, cruel to the weak, or less fortunate
- Curses, uses obscene gestures, doesn't see the need to change
- Has contempt for authority figures
- Explodes verbally or physically when angry
- Does not respect your thoughts or opinion
- Only thinks of himself/herself
- Sees the kind or considerate person as a "wimp."

RUDENESS

Your Grade____ **His/Her Grade_____**

7. TRUE LOVE IS NOT SELFISH.

(I Corinthians 13:5)

I (Ryan) want to refer to something my mother often says, "Twenty-four hours a day we walk in love or selfishness. There are only two worlds to choose from. The moment we step out of love, we step right into selfishness, and vice versa." Mom, I believe you're right. True love chooses love over selfishness, even when it is the most challenging and difficult thing we ever do. True love puts aside its own self-interest and focuses on the needs, the desires, and the interests of the other.

The Bible never says that we should "like" each other, but many, many times it commands us to "love" one another. In this society we are trained to want our needs met first and we want the biggest, the best, the newest, the most expensive and we want it all for ourselves. True love re-trains us to focus away from ourselves to someone else. Selfishness will destroy a relationship. See if you are selfish, or if someone else is selfish:

1. Does he/she act like they are the center of the universe?
2. Do they ignore others?

3. Are they totally self-absorbed?
4. Want you to drop everything to solve his/her problem?
5. Does not offer words of encouragement, praise, or comfort to others?
6. Attempts to control others into submission by whining and complaining to get their way?
7. Do they most often act in love or selfishness?

SELFISHNESS

My Grade_____ His/Her Grade_____

8. TRUE LOVE IS NOT EASILY ANGERED.

(I Corinthians 13:5)

One of the most difficult personality types in relationships is the person who is easily angered or offended. Their anger may be silent and seething or explosive and violent. Either way they have not allowed love to master their tendency to erupt in anger. Anger in, and of itself, is not wrong. We all get angry. Anger is a natural emotion and function. Anger is *wrong* when it is destructive, attacking, and unresolved.

The secret to handling anger in a godly, loving way is found in Ephesians 4:29 –32. These verses say when we are angry we shouldn't "run off at the mouth" and intentionally hurt another with our words. It further states we should forgive quickly, put away bitterness, wrath, and evil speaking. Then be kind, tenderhearted, and forgiving as Christ forgives us.

1. Do you shout, throw, or punch things - become physical when you are angry?
2. Are you an angry person? Do you have difficulty controlling your anger - then cannot seem to put it away?
3. Do you get angry then pout for days?
4. Are you touchy, easily offended, get your feelings hurt often?
5. Is it difficult for you or him/her to ask for, or get forgiveness?
6. Do you want to punish the person who has made you angry – withdrawing from them? Giving them the silent treatment?
7. Do you forgive and forget quickly?

NOT EASILY ANGRY

My Grade______ **His/Her Grade_____**

9. TRUE LOVE FORGIVES.

(I Corinthians 13:6)

Isn't forgiveness a wonderful thing? Where would we be if Christ had not forgiven us of all our sins? Yet, in relationships we can be so judgmental and far from forgiving. True love feels the hurt and the pain of another's failures, and instead of ridiculing them, love is willing to pray and protect the person from further harm. Love seeks to protect, not expose. It would never tell others about the failure or wrong. In fact true love is so merciful that it actually feels the pain and is willing to take the pain upon itself.

This doesn't mean that we should overlook a person's shortcomings, but it does mean that real love will believe and hope the best for that person and freely forgive them for not being perfect.

1. What is your first reaction when you hear of someone else's mistake?
2. Do you forgive easily?
3. Do you think the worst of people or even gloat over their failures?

4. Do you try to soothe and comfort those who have fallen – try to protect them from further harm or ridicule?
5. Are you willing to help bear the burden or hurts that the person may be carrying?
6. Are you merciful, or critical when others mess up?

FORGIVENESS

My Grade______ His/Her Grade_____

10. TRUE LOVE IS TRUTHFUL.

(I Corinthians 13:6)

Many girls believe that most boys lie, but girls are capable of lying as well. It is actually funny that so many girls are determined to understand why boys lie, when instead they should be focusing on why they continually believe them!

We have already discussed in the book the two reasons we lie: 1 – to protect ourselves, then, 2 – to promote ourselves. Either way it leads to unhappy, frustrating relationships. If you are constantly catching the person you are dating in lies, you can bet they would not be different in marriage. We rationalize lying in our society – the little white lies don't matter, we say. Dishonesty always matters.

1. Can he/she be trusted to do what they say?
2. Are they truthful?
3. Do other people believe that he/she tells the truth? Are they respected for their word?
4. Is he/she known for keeping secrets, being trustworthy?
5. Can you depend on the person to tell you the truth about other relationships?
6. Do they keep things from you to "protect" you?
7. Does it seem that they lie when the truth would be easier?
8. Do they lie to enhance their accomplishments, talents, or financial status?

TRUTH

My Grade_____ **His/Her Grade_____**

11. TRUE LOVE BEARS, BELIEVES, HOPES, AND ENDURES.

(I Corinthians 13:7)

Plain and simple, the test of true love is when you are completely loyal to the other person in word and deed. You know it is love when you are committed to making the other person the priority of your life. You *bear* all things with them – that means you will stick with them in good times and bad. True love doesn't quit – you just get up and start all over. True love *believes* they can make it as God works out His plan. True love *hopes* even against the odds and never gives in to despair. You know where you are headed and you are focused on making your relationship and ultimately your marriage all God wants it to be. Lastly, true love *endures*. It stands the test of time. You must give your relationship enough time to divulge all the things you must know. His family/her family – how was he/she raised –with what values, etc. – how are they under pressure, what do they believe spiritually, what kind of parents will he/she be? Have you seen them react in every kind of situation? Does your love endure under pressure? Remember how dinosaurs became extinct? They could not adapt to the world's changing environment. True love adapts no matter what.

1. How does he/she handle pressure? Are they touchy, irritable – or calm and resolved?
2. Does your love bear, believe, hope, and endure through the hard times?
3. Are you committed to loving this person even when they are not at their best, when they are their least attractive, or when you disagree with them?
4. What is your common purpose – have you talked about goals, priorities?
5. Do you know the actions, attitudes, qualities, traits, and abilities that you appreciate most about him/her?
6. Do you see a future with this person - or are you really just having fun dating and have no intention for anything more?
7. Would this person give you loving support and be a "rock" to you during health problems, dire financial stress, and emotional upheaval? How would they react?

LOYALTY

My Grade_____ **His/Her Grade_____**

SO????

To Tie The Knot? – Or Not?

What do you think? Is it true love? Are you clearer than ever about the kind of person with whom you want to spend the rest of your life? How about the person you are dating now? Does he or she fall short in any of these areas? How about you? Do you see the things you need to work on or change about yourself before you become "marriage material?"

Chances are if you are a Christian you have already sensed if the relationship is right, or if there is something wrong. The Spirit of God who is alive in you discerns danger and warns you again and again. Or you may have a deep, settled peace that all is well and there is freedom to proceed in the relationship. *Above all, seek that peace.* If it isn't there, do not lie to yourself or to the other person. To continue in a relationship that we *know* is not God's will is to end up hurt or hurting another. Worse, we live the lie for one reason or another right into marriage and that marriage is programmed to fail. The Apostle Paul stated in Colossians 3:15 to, *"let the PEACE of God RULE in your hearts."* That is the final test – is there peace about your relationship? Let peace, or the lack of peace be your guide.

This is the rest of your life we are talking about. Really think about your current situation and don't rush into the next 40 or 50 years of your life without a peace about the one with whom you'll be spending those years.

We will be praying for you!

Please pray the following as you trust God with your relationships...

"Father,
Thank you for the opportunity to learn about whom You want me to marry and spend my life with. I ask that You would help me to apply the principles I have learned in this book to my life and choose to follow You and trust You with everything.
In Jesus' name.
Amen"

FOOTNOTES

1. *The 10 Commandments of Dating*, by Ben Young. Thomas Nelson Publishing, 1999, Nashville, Tennesse.

2. *Love Takes Time,* by Harvey Corwin. Hope For The Family Publishing, 1999, 1245 South Pine, Canby, Oregon 97013.

3. *11 Reasons Families Succeed,* by Richard and Rita Tate. Hensley Publishing, 2002, Tulsa, Oklahoma.

4. *Unpack The Baggage - Part 5,* by John Mark. John Mark Ministries Publishing. 7 Bangor Court, Heathmont, Australia 3135.

5 & 6. *The Starter Marriage and the Future of Matrimony,* by Pamela Paul. 2000. Villard Books.

7. *Sex In America: A Definitive Survey,* by Robert Michael. The Social Organization of Sexuality and Sexual Practices in the United States. Chicago University Press, 1994, Chicago, Illinois 34985.

8. *Finding the Love of Your Life,* by Neil Clark Warren. Focus On The Family Magazine, June 1992. Colorado Springs, Colorado 89056.

9, 10, & 11. *11 Reasons Families Succeed,* by Richard and Rita Tate. Hensley Publishing, 2002, Tulsa, Oklahoma.

12. *The Myths of Sex,* by Jim Long in Campus Life Magazine, (February 1986).

13. *Unpack The Baggage - Part 5,* by John Mark. John Mark Ministries Publishing. 7 Bangor Court, Heathmont, Australia 3135.

14. *Commitment and the Modern Union: Assessing the Link Between Premarital Cohabitation and Subsequent Marital Stability,* by Neil G. Bennett, Ann Klimas Blanc, and David E. Bloom, American Sociological Review 53, 1988.

15. *Wild at Heart,* by John Eldredge. Copyright 2001. Thomas Nelson Publishers 2001. 501 Nelson Place, Nashville, Tennessee, 37214.

16. *The Number of Couples Cohabitating Soars As Mores Relax,* by Barbara Vobejda. The Houston Chronicle, December 5, 1996. The Houston Chronicle, 234 Main Street Drive, Houston, Texas 74593.

17. *The Myths of Sex,* by Jim Long in Campus Life Magazine, (February 1986).

18. *Studies in the Greek New Testament,* by Kenneth Weust. 1964, Word Publishing, Waco, Texas.

19 & 20. *Living Together,* by Mark Lambert 1998, Hughes Publishing.

21. ICR Survey Research Group poll for USA Weekend by Tom McNichol, "*Sex Can Wait,*" USA Weekend, (March 25-27, 1994, pp. 4-6).

22. *Sex and Marriages,* by George Martin. Summit Ministries, 1998, Gilbert, Arizona 85299.

RESOURCES

Brave New World, by Aldous Huxley. Copyright 1932, 1946, 1958 by Harper & Row Publishers, Incorporated. 10 East 53rd Street, New York, New York 10022.

Don't Let Jerks Get The Best Of You, by Dr. Paul Meier. 1993 Thomas Nelson Publishers, 501 Nelson Place, Nashville, Tennessee, 37214.

His Needs, Her Needs, by Willard Harley. Marriage Builders Publishing, Inc. 1988. White Bear Lake, Minnesota.

Lady In Waiting, by Debbie Jones and Jackie Kendall. Destiny Publishers, 1998. Shippensburg, Pennsylvania.

My Life and the Story of the Gospel Hymns, by Ira Stankey. Philadelphia, Pennsylvania: The Sunday School Times Company, (1907, p. 122).

Oswald Chambers, by E. - Harry Verploegh. Thomas Nelson Publishers, 1987. Nashville, Tennessee.

Personality and Social Psychology Review, by Eliot R. Smith. Journal Press, November 2001, 10 Industrial Avenue, Mahwah, New Jersey, 07430.

Saving Your Marriage Before It Starts, by Dr. Les Parrot and Dr. Leslie Parrot. 2000 P.O. Box 87742, Vancouver, Washington 98687.

Sex At Its Best: Abstinence Without Lust, by Gerald W. Henry. Maturion Media Press, Columbia, Maryland 21045.

The Battle For The Family, by Tim LaHaye. Fleming H. Revell Company, Old Tappan, New Jersey.

The Day America Told The Truth, by James Patterson and Pete Kim. Copyright 1991. New york: Prentice Hall Press.

The English Greek Lexicon, editor James Gall. Baker Book House, 1975. Grand Rapids, Michigan 49530.

The Handfasting Ceremony, by Fr. Sean Colman, Lindisfarne Catholic Church Riverside, California, 1988.

The Living Together Trap, by Rosanne Rosen. New Horizon Press, 1993. Far Hills, New Jersey.

The Marriage Savers, by Michael McManus. Zondervan Publishing, 1995. 5300 Patterson, SE, Grand Rapids, Michigan 49530. All Rights Reserved.

The Odyssey, by Homer. Translated by Samuel Butler. All Rights Reserved, M.I.T. Press, Five CambridgeCenter, Cambridge, Massachusetts 02142, 1954.

The New Virginity, Newsweek Magazine, December 2001, by Lorraine Ali and Julie Scelfo. 251 West 57th Street, New York, New york 10019.

The Science Citation Index Report, by Sir Roy Calne. Cambridge University Press England, 1997, All Rights Reserved.

The Selected Correspondence of Karl Menninger, by Howard J. Faulkner and Virginia Pruitt. 1997. The University of Missouri Press, 2910 LeMone Avenue, Columbia, Missouri 65201.

The Top Ten Relationship Skills, by Rinatta Paries. The Relationship Coach Publishing Company, 2001. P.O. Box 87742, Vancouver Washington 98687.

The United Methodist Church News, June 2000, by Franklin Olson. Memorial Drive United Methodist Chruch, 12955 Memorial Drive, Houston, Texas 77079.

The Woman's Study Bible, by E. - Dorothy Kelley Patterson and Rhonda Harrington Kelley. Thomas Nelson Publishers, 1995. Nashville, Tennessee.

Think On These Things, by John Maxwell. Thomas Nelson Publishers, 1998. 501 Nelson Place Nashville, Tennessee 37214.

Webster's Encyclopedic Unabridged Dictionary, All Rights Reserved 1996. Lithium Distribution Press, Random House Publishers, 235 Park Avenue South, New York, New York 10003.

Why Wait?, by Dr. Elizabeth Whelan, Haversham Press, 1998, New York City, New York.